Minutes with God

Minutes with God

Ricky Lopez

XULON PRESS

Xulon Press
2301 Lucien Way #415
Maitland, FL 32751
407.339.4217
www.xulonpress.com

Printed in the United States of America.

ISBN-13: 978-1-6312-9721-2

Contents

Contents

Endorsements

E xploration. The word evokes a sense of adventure, excitement, challenges, setbacks, thrills, mystery, and astonishments. It is an excursion where one becomes familiar with the unfamiliar. It deals with discovery and a personal experience. The book *Minutes with God* is an aid in taking such important steps on a great expedition of knowing God. It is written by my friend and brother Ricky Lopez, who has been in pursuit of knowing more about his heavenly Father ever since he repented and found true hope in a jail cell. Ricky's exploration has had its difficulties, steep mountains, pits that can encourage many who want to give up and not look to God. In the pursuit of following God, Ricky has given others hope and confidence that God is the answer to life's most difficult problems. I invite you to join in this exploration by meditating and applying the important truth found in *Minutes with God*.

As Ricky has once said, "If it takes a community to convict a person, then it will take a community to help restore a person." May this book help you get into a deeper relationship with God and help you build up the community around you.

Retired Salvation Army Officer/Chaplain
Author: Filthy Rags
Major Tom Ford

Ricky Lopez is one of those amazing Christians who effortlessly and naturally makes the world a better place. From his positive attitude to the strength of his character to the depth of his heart for people, he truly is an authentic follower of Jesus Christ. His first book, *Attitude Reflecting Character,* offered a glimpse into his soul-winning passion and into the wondrous and transformative working of the Holy Spirit in a person's life. No matter where you have been, no matter what you have done, and no matter what has been done to you, God can save and shape you in profound ways. Now, with the much-anticipated publication of *Minutes with God,* we have an excellent and thought-provoking forty-five-day devotional designed to help you spend quality time with your Savior and put your true faith into real action. Indeed, this book will help you grow deeper in your Christian faith and go further in your walk with Jesus!

Dr. Philip W. Calvert, Senior Pastor
Trinity SBC
Casa Grande, Arizona

In my role as a United Methodist Minister I had the opportunity to sit on a Salvation Army Corps Advisory Board. In my association with that board I came to know Ricky Lopez, who served in the role of a youth minister for the Salvation Army West Valley Corps. I found Ricky to be a fine young man with a love of God and a desire to share that love with the young people of our community. Ever since I have known Ricky, I have seen how he spends his life trying to spread his love of Jesus to all who will listen. My hope and prayer are that through this book of devotions Ricky will be able to help the reader grow in their faith and love of Jesus. May this book bring glory to our Lord.

Rev. Louie Lyon
Dove of the Desert United Methodist Church

Dedication

This book is dedicated to you, the reader, and those who invested in it. God cares that we join together to make a difference in the world that we live in. I also would like to dedicate this book to my two sons, Gabriel and Gideon, and my daughter, Grace. My hope is that all my kids would learn how to keep God first and to make an impact for the generations to come. To my lovely wife, I thank you for helping me to stay on track, for loving me, and for helping me to prioritize. Thank you all for taking the time to read this book. To God be the glory and honor in Jesus name. Amen!

Introduction

I f you picked up a copy of this book, you might be wondering what this book has to offer you. In short, it may have nothing to offer you, but if you spend time with God through this book, it has plenty to offer you. In our society, we have invested our time and faith in public education, government officials, or the stock market, but if the truth be told, our time and faith in God is what really matters. In simple terms, spending time with God is like a gym membership, the more you use it, the better results you will begin to have. You cannot go wrong by putting your time in God, but you can go wrong by ignoring Him.

In the following pages you will discover devotional tools, testimonies and pastoral perspectives of what time in God Has shown others. As you read may you be strengthened empowered to be all that Christ would have of you.

Form and Void

I t's amazing to me how the heart and character of God can be seen within the first few scriptures of the Bible. Immediately, God deals with the issue of form and the issue of when a thing is void.

> *"The earth was without form and void, and darkness was over the face of the deep. And the Spirit of God was hovering over the face of the waters." (Gen. 1:2)*

Just like in the beginning of the world, God knows how to bring life, purpose, and beauty in a place that is void and without form. The same is true when we are spiritually empty inside and in need of fulfillment. Sometimes when life seems dark because of the void, or gap between man and God, God is not absent. Likewise, God is not dull or dry in His creativity and personality toward us. When the earth was void and without form, God saw the situation, took action in the situation, and creatively gave life to it. God is at the center of the entire existence of humanity and of humanity's purpose. The fingerprints of God are evident because God is in the details of what He has created. More importantly, when we feel empty, God uses His creativity and presence in our lives to comfort us and to fill us. If God took care of the world in the beginning, how much more do you think He will take care of you? God is not carless about His creation, and when life seems dark, empty and formless, God is still at work. God is a God of order, and a part of His order is to help arrange the things in our life that matter the most. If you have an issue that is making you feel empty or out of order, then it's time to look to God and to be filled. Go back to the root of your issue, and let God be on your side and you on His side.

Reflection

Did you know that God cares about the emptiness you feel and how your spiritual life is being formed? If you are wrestling with an issue, don't turn away from God but toward Him. The enemy would love to have you distracted, panicked, and stressed, but the devil can't take away what you sacrifice and let go of for God.

Prayer

Father God, please fill me up with more of Jesus! You care about me, and I don't want to be defeated and reckless. I want victory and salvation. Save me today from myself. In Jesus name I pray. Amen!

Scripture

For this is what the Lord says—he who created the heavens, he is God; he who fashioned and made the earth, he founded it; he did not create it to be empty, but formed it to be inhabited— he says: "I am the Lord, and there is no other. (Isa. 45:18)

Original Intentions

D id you know that God formed you in your mother's womb with great intention and purpose? Although we have been created with great care, we sometimes misbehave with bad intentions. Originally in the garden of Eden, Adam and Eve had a God-given purpose in life, but when sin came into the world through their disobedience, life became distorted (Gen. chapters 1–3). What was once natural became unnatural through the effect of sin. However, God's intention never changed. God still wanted fellowship with His creation, but man detoured from God's original intentions and plan. In fact, man turned to self-gratification and sinful pleasure while reaping the consequences of sin until this very day. Just as in the beginning, we as humans tend to tamper with God's original intentions and plan for us. For this reason, humanity continues to get in trouble. Man should never change or tamper with the original intentions of God's plan and especially when God has a better life to offer. Exchanging the original intentions of God for polluted intentions or perverted acceptance is not acceptable to God. The Bible calls such practice sin. In today's society such is the case and should not be viewed with offense but in reflection to Gods truth. Modern examples are observed in the behavior of those seeking a sex change for a new identity, or when women aggressively fight for the role of being a man to show independence or authority. However, such philosophy is not God's original intention, and there are eternal consequences for trespassing against Him. A man is a man and was created to be a man on purpose and for a purpose. Likewise, a woman is a woman and was created to be a woman for a purpose and on purpose. We should always know our place in society, at home, or in our environment from God's perspective, not our own desires. God's truth is not hate speech; it's just where honesty for original intention begins! Many people will frown at God's plan when following it, but responsibility and loyalty should always be a priority. God knows our intentions and will deal with us according to our disobedience or repentance. God wants the world to be a better place, and if we follow His intended plan for our lives, we can help and spiritually benefit at the same time. Until Christ returns, we must do our part and respectfully remind others of God's original intention for us.

Reflection

Are you living out God's plan for your life? If not then why not? God has a plan for you, and He wants you to know it. Therefore, keep on studying, praying, and following God until He returns. The Israelites detoured many times in following God, and the consequences of their actions showed. Today, I want to encourage you to share this devotion with someone and discuss it.

Prayer

Father God, thank you for life today. As I think about You, I ask that You clarify Your plan for my life and push me in the right direction. Please make me aware of my surroundings, and may Your purpose for my life encourage me to follow You. Please help me and guide me today. In Jesus name I pray. Amen!

Scripture

"Many are the plans in the mind of a man, but it is the purpose of the Lord that will stand." (Prov. 19:21)

"For I know the plans I have for you, declares the Lord, plans for welfare and not for evil, to give you a future and a hope." (Jer. 29:11)

The Will of God

Have you ever wanted to know what the will of God is? If someone asked you today what the will of God is, what would you tell them? You may have heard many answers to what the will of God is for your life, but do you actually know the biblical answer? The truth is that the will of God is in some way colorful; it is the purpose and plan of God lived out in many ways. The will of God is detailed, and throughout the Bible, it is relational between God and His creation. Scripture helps us to understand that the will of God is like one giant collage centered on the goodness and the nature of God. Since everything begins with God, we find our purpose in God. For clarification read the following scriptures.

1 Thessalonians 5:18

"Give thanks in all circumstances; for this is the will of God in Christ Jesus for you."

1 Peter 2:15

"For this is the will of God, that by doing good you should put to silence the ignorance of foolish people."

Galatians 1:3–5

"Grace to you and peace from God our Father and the Lord Jesus Christ, who gave himself for our sins to deliver us from the present evil age, according to the will of our God and Father, to whom be the glory forever and ever. Amen.

John 7:17

"If anyone's will is to do God's will, he will know whether the teaching is from God or whether I am speaking on my own authority."

Hebrews 10:36

"For you have need of endurance, so that when you have done the will of God you may receive what is promised."

Romans 12:2

"Do not be conformed to this world, but be transformed by the renewal of your mind, that by testing you may discern what is the will of God, what is good and acceptable and perfect."

John 6:40

"For this is the will of my Father, that everyone who looks on the Son and believes in him should have eternal life, and I will raise him up on the last day."

Today, let us be reminded of the will of God and the different ways of uniting in the will of God. Know what the will of God is so that when you pray for the will of God to be done, you pray in agreement with God.

Reflection

Are you desiring to have your will be done in life or God's will to be done in your life? Today, challenge yourself to study the scripture verses shared in this devotion and examine how you can more actively participate in God's plan for your life today.

Prayer

Thank you, God, for wanting to be relational with me and for having my best interest at hand. Please help me to better understand what you are wanting from me and please help me do my best. I want your will in my life and the strength to do what's right. Help me today, in Jesus name. Amen!

Scripture

Ephesians 5:17

"Therefore do not be foolish, but understand
what the will of the Lord is."

Not Ashamed

D o you remember the last time that you were embarrassed? How did it make you feel? Did it make you feel awkward, self-conscious, uncomfortable, or maybe even sheepish? When we are embarrassed, we sometimes try to avoid being seen. Like a turtle, we may want to hide from our situation until we are comfortable and confident enough to face it. On the other hand, we can get protective or even try to create a distraction, but whatever the case may be, we must be truthful about it and be more concerned about what God thinks of us rather than what anyone else does. In my early days of Christianity, I used to be embarrassed to share my faith with certain people because I thought I would be ridiculed, rejected, or made fun of, but little did I know that honoring God was far better than catering to my image or trying to gain approval of anyone. Apparently, I wasn't as surrendered as I thought or hoped to be. I wanted Christianity without a cross or any kind of rejection, but that's not how it works. That's like saying, "I want to be a politician and have everyone agree with me," but that's just not how it works. When we become Christians, we shouldn't seek the approval or acceptance of anyone but God. When we try to fit in with the crowd or become embarrassed at the name of Jesus Christ, we distort the image of Christianity and then deal with a bigger issue of not being surrendered. After all, most issues are resolved in the life of a Christian when real surrender begins. When a Christian is surrendered to God, you can notice a great deal of the beauty found in that person's personality and see a great deal of joy in how that person is unashamed in the mighty name and character of Jesus Christ.

"For I am not ashamed of the gospel, for it is the power of God for salvation to everyone who believes, to the Jew first and also to the Greek." (Rom. 1:16)

Sadly, some professing Christians avoid God when they become embarrassed or ashamed of Him, but they run to Him when they are in need of His refuge and salvation. In such cases one must reconsider why they are acting like that and then decide to get better or to stay tangled up in such disrespect toward God. Today, too many people care about how they look and about who will accept them, so they pretend to be something that they're not instead of sons and daughters that God created them to be. However, nothing will save them from themselves until they get real with themselves and real about their relationship with God. The truth is that there are not enough cosmetics, surgeries, or jewelry in the world for anyone to cover up who they truly are apart from God. It is only when a person can get real about who they truly are that they can sincerely begin the process of confessing their need for God and start seeking His help. Overall, if our concern is in how we look and how sexy we can be, then we only prove to be egotistic and self-centered. In the world that we live in today, a man or woman might get some attention by how he or she looks, but with God what good does that really do? If we are not doing what we are intended to be doing, then we are missing out on the bigger picture and only proving to be small thinkers. The reality behind appearance is that it doesn't attract God, and it will only bring trouble for the individual who uses it for promiscuous and rebellious living. On the other hand, those who pursue intoxication, sexual seduction, and greed, are only misleading others and only building judgment against themselves. However, if repentance is sought, then that person will find favor with God and may even be able to help others. God is serious about the image He created us in, and more importantly, what we do with it. For any one of us, we are held responsible for our actions, words, and the choice to acknowledge God.

"So everyone who acknowledges me before men, I also will acknowledge before my Father who is in heaven, [33] but whoever denies me before men, I also will deny before my Father who is in heaven." (Matt. 10:32–33)

There are consequences for rejecting God. With God we get way more good than what we deserve, but by rejecting Him, we may be on a road of getting what we deserve if we continue to allow embarrassment, shamefulness, and a lack of acknowledgment be the cause of our denial of Him.

Reflection

Have you ever been embarrassed or ashamed to acknowledge God? Are you ever ashamed to say that you love Jesus or afraid to say that you are a Christian? Are you the kind of person that looks good on the outside but is hiding a lot of sin on the inside? If you have been trying to look like a Christian but are not a Christian, then today ask God for His forgiveness for your sins and repent from any evil or manipulation that is in your heart. Begin to work on the very thing that you are convicted of doing wrong and begin to replace any bad habits with Godly living.

Prayer

Father God, may my trust and surrender be found in You. May I truly understand what it means to be under Your care and in the refuge of the cross. I want to recognize that it is you at work in me to do good and to live right. I admit that heaven and salvation are not a fashion show but a life of obedience and sincere faith. I place my trust and concerns in your hands today. Save me from myself. In the mighty name of Jesus Christ I pray. Amen.

Scripture

Psalm 37:5 (ESV)

"Commit your way to the Lord; trust in him, and he will act."

Day 5

Comfort

D id you know that comfort helps to take away
pain? Just as when a child hurts themselves, a
parent's comforting touch can help relieve the pain.
Even as adults we are sometimes like that; we look
for comfort to take away our emotional and physical
pain. We desire comfort to help us cope with whatever
is hurting us. Some people look for comfort in other
people, liquor, sex, eating, prescriptions and so on, but
it is through God Almighty that real healing takes place.
We are creatures of comfort, and that's why we search
for it and yield to it. In the Bible God is known by His
characteristic of comfort, and it is through Him we can
lay our burden of trouble down.

2 Corinthians 1:3–4

Blessed be the God and Father of our Lord Jesus
Christ, the Father of mercies and God of all
comfort, who comforts us in all our affliction, so
that we may be able to comfort those who are

**in any affliction, with the comfort with which we
ourselves are comforted by God.**

There is power in comfort. When used as an evangelistic tool, it can lead to genuine breakthrough. Yes, we need comfort for our pain; and, yes, we need to give comfort to those in pain. The comfort of love, hope, and joy is so powerful that the devil dislikes when we use it. Therefore, let someone know that they are loved by how much you care, not just by what you say. Comfort is relational and is better understood in proximity. Comfort is a pain reliever, and with it our world can change. God wants to comfort us with His presence and through the ministry of His love. The Bible makes it clear that God is the God of all comfort, and if we ignore Him, we will miss our blessing that the comfort of God can provide. Today, many people are still in pain, but today and right now that doesn't have to be us! In Jesus name we can ask God for comfort because that is what a good shepherd does for His flock. When you are hurting, turn to God, He knows how to comfort best.

Reflection

Did you know that God helps to heal a broken world through comfort? God wants us to know Him in a comforting way as well as through our prayer life, studies and worship. Comfort is one of the greatest experiences that we can have and give. If you want to be a better friend, parent, coworker, or whatever you are called to, then care enough to comfort others when needed. Today, if given the chance, comfort someone by encouragement, kind words, scripture, or however God leads you.

Prayer

Father God, I don't want to be rude or bashful; I do want a heart that beats for you. Help me toDay to be more like you. Allow me to comfort those who need comfort as you have comforted me. Let me not speak of comfort but not give it. Teach me today, in Jesus name I pray. Amen!

Scripture

"Even though I walk through the valley of the shadow of death, I will fear no evil, for you are with me; your rod and your staff, they comfort me" (Ps. 23:4).

"From A Pastor's Perspective on Relationships"

by
Rev. Louie Lyon, United Methodist Pastor

If we ever needed to strengthen the institution of family, now is the time. It seems to me there are no absolutes, not even God. Immorality abounds. Listening and hearing one another seems to be a lost art in many homes. Spouses often seem to be going in opposite directions. Parents and children have a hard time communicating. It seems that the modern home is nothing more than a large telephone booth where arrangements are made but relationships are sort of left outside the booth. My wife says to me on occasion "pick up the phone to talk to someone, don't just send a text or email." She tells me that my personal contact leaves something to be desired.

In Luke 12:49–56 we have a troubling text where Jesus says, "I came to bring fire to the earth, and how I wish it were already kindled! Do you think that I have come to bring peace to the earth? No, I tell you but rather division! From now on five in one household will be divided, three against two and two against three..." At first glance this sure doesn't seem like a way to focus on good family relationships, does it? But it gets worse, for Jesus goes on to say they will be divided: father against son and son against father, mother against daughter and daughter against mother. It goes further, which makes one think that Jesus advocates for destruction and division. But dear ones, one of the primary purposes of fire is to cleanse and purify. Divisions may come, but God's first purpose in sending fire to families is to cleanse and purify people's lives and relationships.

Let's look at God's intention of establishing family ties. God created male and female and established marriage and family. God said, "It is good." Family ties are more than human contracts; they are part of God's order. Psalm 68:6 says, "God sets the lonely in families..." Our most fundamental loneliness is only fulfilled by a relationship with our Maker, but we have loneliness for human contact as well. In other words, it's God's intention to give us a preview of fulfillment as members of his eternal family by placing us in loving family relationships in this life.

Family ties are strengthened when family members love and respect God above everything else and have love and respect for one another. Absolute obedience belongs only to God, but we are called to honor those over us in the Lord (parents) and be honorable to those under us in the Lord (children and grandchildren). Spouses are guided in their relationship by Jesus's words, "Just as I have loved you, love one another" (John 13:34). Prior to entering into the ordained ministry I was an elementary school teacher. A bulletin board I used to put up in the beginning of the school year stated, "CHILDREN LEARN FROM WHAT THEY SEE." What that meant was if a child saw disrespect coming from a parent toward another, "what did the child learn?" The fourth of God's Ten Commandments states that we are to honor our father and mother. To honor means to respect. Respect goes both ways, and one cannot expect respect back if they don't show respect for another.

When I was a young man of twenty-five I had only been married for a little over a year. I was asked by someone at the church where we attended, "What was the most important thing in my life?" I didn't take any time in answering that question: I immediately said, "My wife and baby and then God." You see, I was new in the faith and really hadn't thought it all out. As time went on, I realized that if I placed God first in my life, God would help me with my wife and family, and we would not want for anything.

Family ties and relationships are strengthened when each member of a family makes a commitment to Jesus as their Lord and Savior. When one or more family members are unbelievers, barriers go up, divisions occur,, and estrangements happen.

This is what Jesus means when he talks about family goodbyes. The Gospel of Jesus Christ is good news, but when someone is locked into their sins, they may see it as bad news. The fire of the gospel is intended to cleanse family relationships.

Dear ones, if ever we needed family ties and relationships to be established and strengthened, it's today. Faith in the crucified and risen Lord Jesus Christ will do that. Many of us blame someone else when we need to take responsibility for our own actions. I end this note on relationships by asking you a most important question: Do you place God first in your life? I can guarantee you that if you do, God will help you get the priorities in the proper place, and your relations will strengthen. Give it a try if you haven't already. Who is NUMBER ONE in your life is the question I leave you with.

God's Kingdom and Man's Government

Did you know that God's kingdom consists of His leadership? Sometimes we may think that we can vote God in or vote Him out but God doesn't need our vote, and He doesn't use a ballot box for gaining approval. For this reason, some people dislike God and His authority. Some people want to dictate what God can do, but no one is on His level to do that. God is the highest form of justice and perfection. However, God is also the highest form of love and mercy and knows how to bring balance. Although God has allowed many people to reject Him and to create their own form of government, God is like the superior court for all governments and will one Day exercise a verdict on all issues and practices.

Psalm 22:28

"For kingship belongs to the Lord, and he rules over the nations."

In the case of some government systems and in different times, God has blessed entire nations because of the obedience of those who respect God in a nation. God has servants everywhere and even in government positions that acknowledge His way. As a result of obedience and respect to God, a nation is blessed. America is one of those nations; we are not perfect, but the Founding Fathers didn't ignore God, and therefore they were blessed. The Declaration of Independence acknowledges the nature of God, the US currency acknowledges God, the Pledge of Allegiance acknowledges God, and presidents constantly acknowledge God through many different speeches. The evidence can be seen and has been seen but it is often the believers responsibility to point out such things to remind and edify each other. God works through the people, and that is one way that God governs. Throughout the Bible God reminded the Israelites to follow His precepts and ways, but they did not always and had to live with the consequences of their choices. Today, nothing has changed, and we ought to be careful about the direction we go.

"Blessed is the nation whose God is the Lord, the people whom he has chosen as his heritage!"
(Ps. 33:12)

"If my people who are called by my name humble themselves, and pray and seek my face and turn from their wicked ways, then I will hear from

***heaven and will forgive their sin and heal their
land" (2 Chron. 7:14).***

We may be proud to be a successful nation,
but we must be careful and watchful in what
we do and tolerate. God allowed disobedience
in Israel for a season, and the Israelites felt the
punishment of it. Therefore, we shouldn't think that
we are any different in how God can deal with us.
Overall, God doesn't want us to be impressive as
a nation. He wants us to be obedient and faithful.
Our fleshly and political ability isn't the answer to
our spiritual victory. What many fail to realize is that
our spiritual government is where man's economic
government can be restored, healed, and redeemed.
As children of God and loving citizens to our country,
we should be teaching and reminding others not to
forget God in daily living because God is the solution
to providing real success. To ignore God is to neglect
God and to neglect God is to reject salvation.

Reflection

Are you the kind of Christian that keeps God in the
center of your voting, advocating or the love for your
country? It is important that all governments do right
by their people, but most importantly, it is important
that God is acknowledged and not ignored. Today, I
want to encourage you to study the beliefs of the

Founding Fathers of America and see how the theology of God changed them in their political agendas and principles of America.

Prayer

Father God, thank you for who You are and for wanting us to have life and have it more abundantly. May I conform to your ways at home, in my country, and around my neighbors. Keep us safe and help us all to fix what needs to be fixed until you return. In Jesus name I pray. Amen.

Scripture

"Your kingdom is an everlasting kingdom,
And Your dominion *endures* throughout all generations" (Ps. 145:13).

***

[9] Pray then like this: "Our Father in heaven, hallowed be your name.[a]
[10] Your kingdom come, your will be done, on earth as it is in heaven.
[11] Give us this Day our daily bread, [12] and forgive us our debts,
as we also have forgiven our debtors. [13] And lead us not into temptation, but deliver us from evil (Matt. 6:9–13).

Day 7

Earnest Prayer

H ave you ever prayed for something halfheartedly? Did you know that some people pray out of routine or tradition? As humans, sometimes we pray just to pray so that we can feel better, but when things get tough, we tend to pray the best or the hardest. When praying we should understand that praying is a spiritual conversation with God. Praying is where relationship, intersession, and communication are made between us and God. To pray to God is to believe in God, and in the measure of belief, God is revealed. The stronger the faith you have in God, the stronger your encounters with God become. Praying says a lot about the faith we have in God. For the Christian, there is power in prayer, and when prayer is earnest, the results become greater. When the Apostle Peter was targeted and put in jail, the Bible says that earnest prayer was made for him, and as a result an angel of the Lord set Peter free on an escape route in Acts chapter 12. Maybe sometimes we don't encounter the power of prayer in greater measures because we are not approaching or seeking

God with an earnest heart. The focusing word found in Peter's story (Acts 12) is often "prayer," but the adjective is "earnest." You see, when we are earnest about prayer, results become evident. Not only is it important to pray for yourself, but it is also important that community prays with you or for you.

"Confess your trespasses to one another, and pray for one another, that you may be healed. The effective, fervent prayer of a righteous man avails much" (James 5:16).

In some ways we can be comforted to understand that prayer is part of Gods process to a person's freedom. Sometimes that freedom is a physical freedom or a spiritual freedom if not both. Now in the case of Daniel, it took him to a place of prison/judgment but what was the difference? Daniel was thrown in a lion's den for not changing his prayer life or commitment to God, but not even the lions could harm him (Daniel 6). In scripture God helps us to understand how important a prayer life really is. Today God has given us the name of His son Jesus Christ to pray in because in the name of Jesus, chains are broken, and intersession is made!

"And there is salvation in no one else, for there is no other name under heaven given among men by which we must be saved" (Acts 4:12).

Praying in Jesus name is a great reminder of God's love for us and praying earnestly concretes a greater relationship.

Reflection

How is your prayer life today? Can you improve it? Prayer is so important, and we shouldn't take it lightly. Today, I want to encourage you to have more prayer time with God. Talk to Him and reach out to Him. God wants a better relationship with you. Remember, no matter where you are, you can pray to God, even silently in your mind.

Prayer

Father God, please help me to be more earnest in my prayer life with you. I want to see the impact of prayer result in a greater relationship with you. Bring conviction where I need convicting in my heart and help me to desire more of you. In Jesus name, I pray. Amen!

Scripture

[2] Continue steadfastly in prayer, being watchful in it with thanksgiving. (Col. 4:2)

Day 8

Ways of Obedience

D id you know that obedience can happen in seven different ways? Even though you can add more to this list, I will stop here:

#1. Obedience through inspiration
 # 2. Obedience through conviction
#3. Obedience to the written word of God
#4. Obedience to the audio voice of God
#5. Obedience through love
#6. Obedience to revelation
#7. Obedience to leadership

When thinking about obedience, we can be reminded that there is more than one way for obedience to happen. Obedience is a step closer to godliness. Yes, we may know what to do some of the time, but the truth is that we all need a reminder. Obedience is a general word for God's holistic plan for us, but it suggests two very important things: first, God speaks to us. Second, we have plenty of opportunities to commune with God. Let's look at some of these key ways to walk with God.

First, obedience to inspiration is when you are inspired by God to do something right. God would much rather have you move through motivation and inspiration rather than obligation. God wants you to want Him primarily through desire rather than obligation. When God gives you inspiration to do right with your life it's because He is helping you to move forward in life, not backwards.

Consider 2 Timothy 3:16–17: "All Scripture is breathed out by God and profitable for teaching, for reproof, for correction, and for training in righteousness, that the man of God may be complete, equipped for every good work."

Second, obedience through convictions is when you know what to do through the help of Godly conviction. When we are not supposed to do something, Godly conviction normally warns us in a piercing way. God is gracious to us by helping us to stay out of trouble and by warning us of potential trouble. God is a provider in this way and faithful to help us.

Consider John 16:7–8: "Nevertheless, I tell you the truth: it is to your advantage that I go away, for if I do not go away, the Helper will not come to you. But if I go, I will send him to you. And when he

comes, he will convict the world concerning sin and righteousness and judgment."

Third, obedience to scripture (God's written word) is when we see God's word or hear God's voice for ourselves. It is then at the seeing and hearing of God's word that we are accountable. Yes, we are accountable for ignoring His word as well, but when we see and hear it for ourselves, it becomes more personal. God confronts us with His word versus our own opinions. God wants us to know what He is saying, and through scripture this is one of the ways He does it.

Consider Psalm 119:105: "Your word is a lamp to my feet and a light to my path."

Fourth, obedience to the audio voice of God is a rare thing that happens, but it is very biblical. At certain times you may hear strong testimonies of this happening to people, and if you are such a person to have heard God in this manner, then be very thankful and do as God would have you to do.

Consider: Matthew 3:17: "And a voice from heaven said, "This is my Son, whom I love; with him I am well pleased."

Fifth, obedience through love is purely a heart condition. It's a call to love from the amount of love that you have from God. Your measure of godly love is wrapped in how much you value God. Not all Christians value God in the same way, but all Christians need God. We are not all the same, and we don't love the same. Although we are commanded to love and to exercise this wonderful gift, we do not do it in the same manner or at the same time. Often times Christians may be mistaken by what they do in the name of love, but in the genuine character of love you can notice the difference. God uses love as a powerful tool because it is the unmistakable beauty of Himself being made manifest. For some, the word love holds a big definition and for others it does not. (Read 1 Corinthians 13)

Consider Colossians 3:14: "And above all these put on love, which binds everything together in perfect harmony."

   Sixth, obedience to revelation can be understood as God revealing a message to us or giving us a vision to be fulfilled. Revelation is like an insight of what God is up to and one of the greatest ways that God speaks to His people. The big picture is that God wants you to be in the known of His will and plan and that is often for participation.

Consider Matthew 16:17: "And Jesus answered him, 'Blessed are you, Simon Bar-Jonah! For

**flesh and blood has not revealed this to you, but
my Father who is in heaven.'"**

Seven, obedience to leadership has a lot to do with good stewardship and submission to the order of God. Listening to leadership is an obedience that God uses to help His people grow. We are not our own leaders, and God uses people to help bring direction and caution to our lives through appointed and Christ-led leaders. Recognizing who God uses as leaders is important as well as praying for them and asking God to help. Leaders are never to preach their own agenda but God's. It is always important to ask God who He is using to speak into your life as a leader.

**Consider 1 Thessalonians 5:12–13: "Now we ask
you, brothers and sisters, to acknowledge those
who work hard among you, who care for you in
the Lord and who admonish you. Hold them in
the highest regard in love because of their work.
Live in peace with each other."**

Reflection

After reading today's devotion did you think differently about the many ways you can exercise trust and obedience to God? All that we do is important to God and others. When we truly approach obedience as a way and act of love, we can be very happy to know that a heathy relationship with God exists.

Prayer

Father God, thank you for introducing yourself to me and for making your ways known to me. Help me to walk in all that you would have of me. Change any wrong thoughts in me and grow me up in your ways toDay and now. In the mighty name of Jesus Christ I pray. Amen.

Scripture

As obedient children, do not be conformed to the passions of your former ignorance, but as he who called you is holy, you also be holy in all your conduct, since it is written, "You shall be holy, for I am holy." (1 Pet. 1:14–16, ESV)

Day 9

Image

D id you know that God is more interested in how you live verses how you look? God values your character and intentions more than your clothes or appearance. Our perishable looks don't have eternal purpose. The makeup that women wear or the muscles that men body build for don't impress God. Good looks and self-reputation often lead to pride and pride has no kingdom value.

Proverbs 11:2

"When pride comes, then comes disgrace, but with humility comes wisdom."

Proverbs 16:18

"Pride goes before destruction, and a haughty spirit before a fall."

James 4:6

"But he gives more grace. Therefore it says, 'God opposes the proud but gives grace to the humble.'"

Now don't get me wrong, God loves beautiful things that the eye can see or else He wouldn't have been so artistic about His creation. I have been to plenty of beautiful places in my life, and I know that when I see nature clothed in its beauty that God gave it, I humbly give thanks and admire God even more. However, it is when you or I become self-centered that we begin to insult God. It is disrespectful not to give credit to where credit is due and it is dangerous to put our human image in a higher view than God. We are to be modest when it comes to the beauty that God gives but many have become seducers and prostitutes of their God given beauty.

Proverbs 31:30

"Charm is deceitful, and beauty is vain, but a woman who fears the Lord is to be praised."

Charm and beauty can often be the mask to an ambush but Godly character dose not seek to ambush. Overall, God doesn't want us to be impressive through our looks when we can be world changers through our character in Christ Jesus.

Reflection

Have you ever tried to be impressive by how you look? Is your image and reputation more important than your character? Today, I want to encourage you to repent if this has been a recent issue for you. God's love for you isn't determined by your outward beauty but by His generosity to you. As you think about this, ask God to help you be more modest if pride and self image has been a stronghold in your life.

Prayer

Father God, please help me to turn away from any self-centered attitudes and to be more mindful of being modest and humble. Thank you for loving me and wanting the best for me. In Jesus name I pray. Amen.

Scripture

1 Peter 3:3–4

[3] Do not let your adorning be external—the braiding of hair and the putting on of gold jewelry, or the clothing you wear—[4] but let your adorning be the hidden person of the heart with the imperishable beauty of a gentle and quiet spirit, which in God's sight is very precious.

Day 10

Good or Perilous Times

Too often we use the word *good* loosely. We sometimes intentionally think that bad things can be called good, but in truth, God is good, Bad is bad. The Bible makes it clear that such times will come that people will call evil good. For example, people call rated R movies good. They call their party or club life good. They call their intoxicating drinks good. They call their sexual sin outside of marriage good. They call themselves good. They call bad things good because they do not understand what good really is. Good is not based on a one-time experience, it is based on truth. The Bible makes it clear that God is good, and in God's goodness His holiness is discovered.

Isaiah 5:20

"Woe unto them that call evil good, and good evil; that put darkness for light, and light for darkness; that put bitter for sweet, and sweet for bitter!"

Again, the Bible makes it clear that God is good, and for some that might be scary because that means that God will have to deal with them without compromising His standard of Justice. God is who defines the standard of good, not our opinions. We may be able to describe attributes of good, but until we taste and see that God is good we won't really understand the true standard of what good really is. We need to experience it, not just hear about it.

Psalm 34:8

"Oh, taste and see that the Lord is good! Blessed is the man who takes refuge in him!"

In the world we live in, we must keep watch over our lives and understand that the evil we see is not the definition of good but the indicator of perilous times.

2 Timothy 3:1–7

"This know also, that in the last days perilous times shall come.

² For men shall be lovers of their own selves, covetous, boasters, proud, blasphemers, disobedient to parents, unthankful, unholy,

³ Without natural affection, trucebreakers, false accusers, incontinent, fierce, despisers of those that are good,

⁴ Traitors, heady, high minded, lovers of pleasures more than lovers of God;

⁵ *Having a form of godliness, but denying the power thereof: from such turn away.*

⁶ *For of this sort are they which creep into houses, and lead captive silly women laden with sins, led away with divers lusts,*

⁷ *Ever learning, and never able to come to the knowledge of the truth."*

Reflection

Have you ever mistaken the definition of good for a lie? Today, I want to encourage you to rethink the word *good* and why it may be wrong to loosely use it. Share this devotion with someone and discuss your thoughts.

Prayer

Father, thank you for being the standard of what good really is. In Your goodness holiness in present. In Your goodness Your character is truly exalted. Praise, honor, and gratitude truly belong to you. Work on me toDay and help me to know you better. In Jesus name. Amen.

Scripture

Romans 12:21

²¹ Do not be overcome by evil, but overcome evil with good.

Obedience and Inspiration

An important thing to know about Christianity is that God speaks loudly through inspiration. It's not a mistake to feel inspiration from the Lord. The only mistake with having divine inspiration is when one ignores it. You see, God gives inspiration, but obedience is up to us. When God inspires a man, He has provided direction for that man and has given a hand of opportunity. When we are stirred up by God, prompted by God, or motivated by God, it is because God is at work in us. Like the wind, we cannot see it, but we can feel it, and we can see what it does to the environment around us. The same impact is true in terms of inspiration: we cannot see it coming our way, but when it does, we can feel it and see what it's doing in the lives of others when others obtain and obey how God is using it. Some of us may understand that inspiration is the process of being mentally stirred up to action or to creativity, but in either case, God uses inspiration to move His people. Sometimes we need help, and godly inspiration is one way God is helping us to get on the right track. For centuries God has inspired men to get involved in His will, but being inspired and not becoming involved is a choice that each of us have to make.

Reflection

Have you ever gone to church and been inspired to live a better life for God? If so, what was your result? Did you know that inspiration is a tool for your benefit and one way that God speaks to you? Remember, you are loved by God, so be motivated and encouraged to make great and impacting decisions .

Scripture

2 Timothy 3:16

"All Scripture is God-breathed and is useful for teaching, rebuking, correcting and training in righteousness,"

Prayer

God, it is my prayer that I am not stubborn when you inspire me to press in and make decisions. May I choose obedience when I am inspired by you and not excuses of the things I can't do without you. May I exercise the faith that you have given me. In Jesus name I pray. Amen!

Importance of Attitude and Character

Did you know that your attitude in life can affect your relationships in life? Your attitude reflects your character, and your character is what people like or dislike. More importantly, how God sees your character is what counts the most. In life, our character says a lot about our spiritual condition and the way we think. Likewise, if our attitude is wrong, it's an indicator that our thinking and character are wrong. Our attitude may help strengthen future opportunities in life, but ultimately it is our character that is the vehicle that drives us there. God wants us to have a good attitude in life because God cares about the relationships we make and how we witness to others. We should never treat others based on how we feel about them but on what is right accordingly to the character of Jesus Christ, who is our greatest example.

Romans 12:18

"If it is possible, as far as it depends on you, live at peace with everyone."

Yes, it is true that not everyone is going to like you but how you live now may help change the way others might persecute or treat you tomorrow.

As Christians it is important to note that if we are always having a bad Day and never joyful, something is wrong. More importantly, love, joy, and peace are a huge part of the fruit of the spirit, which testifies to our right-now condition.

Galatians 5:22–23

[22] "But the fruit of the Spirit is love, joy, peace, patience, kindness, goodness, faithfulness, [23] gentleness, self-control; against such things there is no law."

Your attitude and character matter to God and the world you live in. If you allow your thinking to be affected, then your attitude may expose your character. Yes, it's okay to be honest about our character but not hurtful with it. When in doubt about living right, turn to the example of Jesus.

Reflection

Do you know the importance of your character? Did you know that God cares about how you feel, what you do, and how you treat others? Today, I want to encourage you to work on being a better you. If you know you need improvement then ask God for help and make goals for yourself.

Prayer

Father God, thank you for wanting me to be at my best in life and wanting me as your witness. Help me to be faithful and encouraging to those around me. May I reflect your character in life and not my own agenda. Fill me up with more of you. In Jesus name I pray. Amen.

Scripture

Matthew 5:14

[14] "You are the light of the world. A city set on a hill cannot be hidden."

Day 13

The Flirt to a War Cry

Today, we are going to dip into the story of a man who was a flirt but who later had one of the loudest war cries ever recorded. If you are about the business of making war against the devil, against your flesh, and against your failures, then this devotion is particularly for you. We are talking about a man by the name of Samson. Something important to note about Samson is that he was born to a woman who had been barren up until the time she became informed by an angel of the Lord that she would give birth to a child by the name of Samson. She was also informed that Samson was to be a Nazirite, dedicated to God from the womb (Judges 13). One of the major responsibilities that Samson had by being a Nazirite was not to have a razor touch his head. Basically, this meant that Samson couldn't get a haircut. Yes, this may sound crazy to some, but the practices of being a Nazirite wasn't for a fashion statement but for the discipline and practice of obedience to something greater than self. Another principle found in this story is that when you give your word to God, it is important that you keep your word because obedience is greater than excuses.

"But let your 'Yes' be 'Yes,' and your 'No,' 'No.'
For whatever is more than these is from the evil
one" (Matt. 5:37).

Importantly we as believers must learn how to be more intentional in our communication, whether we are speaking through body language, singing, or using social media as an avenue. As for Samson he grew in obedience to this vow and was given incredible strength from God to be a living testimony among His own people and even the enemies of Israel. However, Samson had a weakness in his mind and heart when it came to women who gave him attention or who flirted with him. Because Samson was strong and had a mighty reputation, maybe some of the women of his Day flirted a little to catch his attention and to seek shelter or prestige with him. Maybe some even wanted to test him, but in all cases, Samson had to make important decisions in his life, just like we do.

"Say to wisdom, "You are my sister," and call
insight your intimate friend, to keep you from
the forbidden woman, from the adulteress with
her smooth words" (Prov. 7:4–5).

Unfortunately, Samson was about to get caught in a mess of his own making. Although he was a giant among the people and feared by how God was working in his life, Samson was about to do the unthinkable with a little bit of persuasion, flirtation, and compromise in the name of love. You see, Samson was an instrument for God to bring judgment by fighting off the enemy camp, so Samson naturally had a contract kill against him. However, men couldn't defeat him in battle because the spirit of the Lord came upon him and did the supernatural through him. Therefore, the enemy camp hired a woman by the name of Delilah to seduce Samson in order to get him to give up the secret of his strength. On three occasions she asked him what the secret was, and Samson gave her false information on each occasion but continued to entertain her in the name of love. Finally, as Delilah kept pestering Samson to tell her the secret of his strength (In the name of love), Samson gave in. Sadly, Samson gave in and compromised. After Samson told Delilah about how he got and kept his strength through his commitment of no razor touching his head, Delilah told the enemy camp, and an ambush to capture Samson was set up. While Samson was sleeping, Delilah cut Samson's hair and Samson was no longer untouchable and was finally captured after Delilah signaled for the arrest. The unfortunate event continued as the enemy camp cut out Samsons eyes and used him as a trophy. While at a large party the Philistines would celebrate the capture of Samson and invite all the people to see what the Philistines had accomplished. In doing this the Philistines displayed Samson as a trophy between two pillars that helped support the building that they all were meeting at. This building would be where the people got to celebrate and amuse themselves at the sight of Samson being defeated. I'm sure that most of the government officials of the Philistines were present and having a fantastic time. Many came to celebrate but unfortunately for them, God wasn't done with Samson, and Samson wasn't done with God.

"Being confident of this, that he who began a good work in you will carry it on to completion until the Day of Christ Jesus" (Phil. 1:6).

You see, Samson was in despair and feeling his failure and the weight of his disobedience. By this time Samson understood clearly that all the torture, ridicule, and regret were all part of the consequence of sin. Samson knew that he had failed but Samson didn't fully give up. Instead of dying as a miserable man in his failures, Samson inwardly looked to God and declared war against the enemy camp. Samson placed his hands on the two nearby pillars and asked God for strength to push the pillars apart and to collapse the building where the thousands of Philistines came to celebrate. For Samson this wasn't suicide; this was an act of war, and God heard Samson's war cry and granted it.

Samson didn't die as a failure—he died as a warrior and displayed a sign against the enemy camp that God stood with the Israelites (Read Judges 13–16 for more details on the life of Samson).

Scripture

"Put on the whole armor of God, that you may be able to stand against the schemes of the devil" (Eph. 6:11).

Reflection

Did you know that war is never pretty? People get hurt intentionally, and many people die and then face eternity while loved ones are stuck at home to deal with the hurt. In the case of Samson, he was at war, and he didn't recognize how powerful the pain of war was until he was captured and tortured. Oftentimes the same is true for us. We don't feel the piercing impact of war until the enemy has really hit us where it hurts. Maybe toDay you don't recognize the war around you in the spiritual realm, or maybe you don't recognize how the enemy is trying to make puppets out of people, but let toDay be the Day to remind you. May you learn to fight in the way God wants you to fight.

Prayer

Father God, may I not forget or neglect my post of duty in this great mission of Christian living. If I forsake anything, then let it be the things that hurt me. May I not be entangled by the affairs of this world but spiritually connected to your leading and not emotionally driven. Help me toDay to persevere in the war against my soul and to preserve with the faith You have given me for such times of need. In Jesus name I pray. Amen.

Day 14

Time

The first time that I ever read Ecclesiastes 3:1–8 I was glad to hear that the Bible talked about everything in life having a time. For me this was helpful because I was horrible in how I spent my time. Like many people today, I have discovered that time management is such an important factor in life. As human beings our days are numbered, and we have to make the most of our time.

> *"See then that you walk circumspectly, not as fools but as wise, 16 redeeming the time, because the days are evil." (Eph. 5:15–16)*

As stewards and members of the body of Christ, we can be challenged by how we spend our time, but we must prioritize our time correctly.

> *12 "Teach us to number our days, that we may gain a heart of wisdom." (Ps. 90:12)*

Sometimes it's better to say no to certain things in life and to readjust our schedule when we are constantly being stretched thin. Making progress at a steady pace is sometimes healthier than running at a full speed recklessly. Spending our time wisely makes a difference. Unfortunately, we're not always intentional about our time because of the various pressures that we face in life, but when it comes to life-threatening issues, we tend to value our time a little bit better. The truth is that we only have so much time here on earth, and then we will have to meet our maker to face judgment. Unfortunately, some have not prepared very well for that important appointment.

> *27 And just as it is appointed for man to die once, and after that comes judgment. (Heb. 9:27)*

We are accountable for what we do with our time. The way we spend it says a lot about what we value. If we are being honest about things, we all make time for what we like or care about. What or who we care about shows. As humans we are limited with the time we have, and our obedience/response to God is a time-sensitive reality. We shouldn't allow certain things to dictate our time with God but we should allow our time with God to show us our true priorities in life.

Reflection

Did you know that how you spend your time is something that the Lord pays attention to? Today, I want to encourage you to take the time to think about how you have been spending your time. Ask God how you should be spending your time and make the changes needed. share this devotion with someone and discuss how you feel about it.

Scripture

1 "There is a time for everything, and a season for every activity under the heavens:
2 a time to be born and a time to die, a time to plant and a time to uproot,
3 a time to kill and a time to heal, a time to tear down and a time to build,
4 a time to weep and a time to laugh, a time to mourn and a time to dance,
5 a time to scatter stones and a time to gather them, a time to embrace and a time to refrain from embracing,
6 a time to search and a time to give up, a time to keep and a time to throw away,
7 a time to tear and a time to mend, a time to be silent and a time to speak,
8 a time to love and a time to hate, a time for war and a time for peace."

(Eccles. 3:1–8)

Prayer

Father God, please help me make the most of my time that I may glorify You best. May I have a heart after Yours and care for the time that You have given me here on earth. May I spend my time to give and not just to take. Please help me to balance what I need to balance and to prioritize the most important things of my days. In Jesus name I pray. Amen.

Start Somewhere

Everything has a starting place, but not everyone may like where they are starting from. Yet, starting in a bad situation doesn't have to turn into a bad finish. As believers we should be concerned about the direction of our life and we should be acknowledging the location and mindset of where we are starting our day-to-Day routines. Some people wake up to a mess from sins committed the night before while others wake up happily in their homes. In any case, the starting place of one thing often sets the stage for other things. This is one reason why we like to start teaching our kids valuable principles early on in life. We understand that decent character is often formed by starting in the right environment and mindset of life. Therefore, if we don't start with God, then we don't have great direction for true success and character. As Christians we need to start our thinking from a Kingdom prospective. We need to get to the gate/heart of the matter and make better decisions.

"I am the gate; whoever enters through me will be saved. They will come in and go out, and find pasture" (John 10:9).

Jesus claimed Himself as the Gate in which He lets in and He lets out. Undoubtedly, the Christian life starts with Jesus. When life gets tough, we must remember that returning to Jesus is our fresh start. When we reevaluate our priorities and put God first, the Gate to better thing begin to open. God knows how to take care of His people, and His love for us has given us the opportunity in life to start, continue, and finish well.

Reflection

Do you know how to get a fresh start in life? Call upon Jesus and ask that you receive a fresh start. Renounce your sins, and confess that Jesus is Lord.

Prayer

Father God, I confess my sins to you and acknowledge that Jesus is Lord. May I have a fresh start with you and help along the way. May my backwards days be put behind me and my forward days in front of me. Thank you, God. In Jesus name I pray. Amen.

Scripture

Proverbs 3:6

6 "in all your ways submit to him,
and he will make your paths straight."

Rehabilitation from a Pastor's Perspective

by
Matthew Thomas

Rehabilitation is probably one of the most misused words in the English language. We use it to represent a variety of things that it doesn't mean. The definition of *rehabilitation* is "the action of restoring someone to health or normal life through training and therapy after imprisonment, addiction, or illness."

We use this word like if it's a cheap band aid that's not going to last very long but there is such a deeper meaning here. Not that these are wrong, but it just cheapens the meaning when we use it frivolously.

Another word this makes me think about is *redemption*. Coincidentally, there are many similarities. The Bible speaks repeatedly about the devastation and destruction of sin that we walk ourselves into, and then when we think that there is no hope, He comes in and redeems the broken and shattered pieces of our lives.

Now, this is not all the time, just a snap of the fingers and BOOM! We are good! Most of the time, it is the process of rehabilitation that reshapes these pieces that we have and starts building, sanding, and shaping the former mess into the most beautiful story ever told.

His Story

"All Scripture is God breathed, and useful for teaching, rebuking, correcting and training in righteousness. So that the servant of God may be thoroughly equipped for every good work" (2 Tim. 3:16–17).

Matthew Thomas
Book Author: The Overlooked

Day 16

Forgiveness and Second Chances for Repentance, Part 1

When I think about forgiveness, I try to remember that Christ died for humanity and the action of that within itself has to deal a lot with the kind of love that offers forgiveness. Yes, this includes forgiveness for the criminal, not just the healthy or wealthy people in life. Although some people may not like to hear this, it still is God's truth.

> *"On hearing this, Jesus said to them, 'It is not the healthy who need a doctor, but the sick. I have not come to call the righteous, but sinners'" (Mark 2:17).*

In terms of forgiveness, it appears that only wrong people need it. Therefore, the truth of the matter is that we all need it because none of us are perfect and at some point, we all have sinned in one way or another.

Romans 3:23

[23] "For all have sinned and fall short of the glory of God."

Sin is unfortunate when it happens, and the result of it is the evidence that we need a savior. No man or woman can inhabit heaven without the forgiveness of their sins. No matter whether we have committed one or ten sins, we need forgiveness if we wish to be clean and redeemed.

"If we confess our sins, he is faithful and just to forgive us our sins and to cleanse us from all unrighteousness" (1 John 1:9).

"He who covers his sins will not prosper, But whoever confesses and forsakes them will have mercy" (Prov. 28:13).

Now let's talk a little bit about what unforgiveness can do.

"And whenever you stand praying, forgive, if you have anything against anyone, so that your Father also who is in heaven may forgive you your trespasses" (Mark 11:25).

"For if you forgive others their trespasses, your heavenly Father will also forgive you, [15] but if you do not forgive others their trespasses, neither will your Father forgive your trespasses" (Matt. 6:14–15).

A big picture in all of this is that our spiritual progress really happens in the forgiveness that God extended to us and our spiritual progress will continue to develop in the exercise of Godly forgiveness.

Scripture

[21] "Then Peter came up and said to him, "Lord, how often will my brother sin against me, and I forgive him? As many as seven times?" [22] Jesus said to him, "I do not say to you seven times, but seventy-seven times." (Matt. 18:21–22).

Reflection

Did you know that Christianity doesn't work without forgiveness being involved? Forgiveness can often be an overlooked word but whether you ask for it or not, it is not overlooked by God. God has a high standard concerning forgiveness because forgiveness is related to the character of God, not a cheap salvation. We need a Godly character and maturity in this truth about forgiveness if we really care about our Christian development.

Prayer

Lord God, please forgive me for my lack of not forgiving others as You have desired from me. I'm not perfect in this matter, but with Your help I can be better, so being better is what I am asking. I understand that I'm being immature when I let unforgiven sins dictate how I feel, so please help me to get any and all unforgiveness out of me. Please forgive me and thank You for what You have done and are about to do. This I pray, In Jesus name. Amen.

Day 17

Forgiveness and Second Chances for Repentance, Part 2

Have you ever wondered what life would be like if second chances didn't exist? Oftentimes we are quicker to accept a second chance but hesitant to offer one to someone else, even when God prompts us to such action. We may even discover disobedience by not forgiving or extending a second chance to others. If God wants us to forgive someone, then who are we to disobey Him? In such a case, the unforgiver will be in need of asking God for forgiveness when he or she becomes too prideful to forgive. Overall, we shouldn't forget that God is the one who sees the bigger picture and has a plan in the course of second chances:

> *15 "See to it that no one fails to obtain the grace of God; that no "root of bitterness" springs up and causes trouble, and by it many become defiled." (Heb. 12:15)*

Sometimes we forget that God died for the worst of the worst of us and when we become unforgiving with those who are sincerely seeking forgiveness, then we become the worst of the worst. The truth is that when a person is seeking forgiveness, then you or I must set aside our ego, emotions and pride because Jesus loves that person and wants the best for that person as well. We must never forget that God is more concerned about salvation rather than focusing on a person's past. The fact that God cares about giving anyone a second, third, or seventy times seven chances is the fact that God loves with a great love. This is good news that is humbling, but apart from God's help we won't get any better or spiritually healthier. Now, don't get me wrong; God has a balance in all of this. If we truly want forgiveness, then we must ask for it and truly repent. God desires repentance.

"I have not come to call the righteous but sinners to repentance" (Luke 5:32).

Taking this a step further, believers aren't perfect and need repentance too. This may sound strange to some, but the truth is that Christians are nothing less than a bunch of forgiven sinners striving to maintain a faithful walk with God. Christians have to ask for forgiveness and keep its fruit because even the best of the best fall short.

16 "For a righteous man may fall seven times and rise again, But the wicked shall fall by calamity. 17 Do not rejoice when your enemy falls, and do not let your heart be glad when he stumbles; 18 Lest the Lord see it, and it displease Him, And He turn away His wrath from him." (Prov. 24:16–18)

8 "Bear fruits in keeping with repentance. And do not begin to say to yourselves, 'We have Abraham as our father.' For I tell you, God is able from these stones to raise up children for Abraham." (Luke 3:8)

19 "Therefore repent and return, so that your sins may be wiped away, in order that times of refreshing may come from the presence of the Lord; 20 and that He may send Jesus, the Christ appointed for you" (Acts 3:19–20)

When a Christian sins, he or she is often known as a backslider and sometimes is mistreated by the church, but realistically, does this really solve anything? This kind of behavior can trigger a weak person to stumble even more. The point is that how we deal with each other is important. If a brother or sister falls, then help them get back up, just don't stare at them in disgust. Overall, God does care about how you or I deal with His beloved.

Reflection

Did you know that forgiven sinners are the ones who go to heaven? How else can anyone get to heaven if they are not forgiven through Jesus Christ? God values second chances and forgiveness, and we must value it as well. God wants a solution to any problem, not the continuation of the problem. ToDay if there is unforgiveness and bitterness in your heart, turn away from it and turn to God for the help needed.

Prayer

Lord God, thank You for offering to me what I don't deserve. Thank you for the cross of Jesus Christ. In my weakness to forgive and show the forgiveness of Jesus Christ, please help me not to fail. Thank you and may my hope and help be in You. In Jesus name I pray. Amen.

Scripture

1 John 1:9

[9] "If we confess our sins, he is faithful and just to forgive us our sins and to cleanse us from all unrighteousness."

Day 18

Work and Responsibility

I t's a beautiful thing to work and help meet the needs of your family. However, not everyone likes to work, and not everyone likes the idea of responsibility. Some people would rather depend on a government system than a moral or biblical principle of earning an honest paycheck. Is it not the Lord who gives us the ability to earn and gain wealth?

> *18 But remember the Lord your God, for it is he who gives you the ability to produce wealth, and so confirms his covenant, which he swore to your ancestors, as it is today. (Deut. 8:18)*

Receiving a handout shouldn't always be the perspective that one lives by. Now for those who really need the help and have the burden of certain disabilities, this isn't to disrespect you. This isn't a teaching aimed at you. On the other hand, this is a stirring of the heart for those who don't bear the weight of a real disability but who intentionally try and cut corners in life by taking advantage of the help that the government system or anyone else has to offer. As an American I can say that the sad truth about this is that those who take advantage of the American government system are the ones robbing their own countrymen who pay taxes. Now you might not have been expecting a devotion like this today, but the truth is that God does care about the economy and our government issues. After all, why wouldn't He care? The Bible is not just about faith talk; it's also about the entire human race and development of it. In terms of work and responsibility, God does not create lazy men—bad choices from men create lazy men. In life, if you want something, you must put in the work, and what you work for is what makes the difference. For example, if you want to use money to party instead of wanting and using money to help provide for your family, then it will show, and you will have to stand before God for your desires and actions. If you want something, then go get it, but do it the right and honest way, even if it's the long way.

Reflection

Did you know that God gives you the ability to produce wealth? Today, be encouraged to pray for a plan to help you and your family financially, spiritually, and holistically. God cares to help you, but be careful how you define success and don't let perishable treasure distract you from a relationship with God.

Scripture

[10] "For even when we were with you, we used to give you this order: if anyone is not willing to work, then he is not to eat, either. [11] For we hear that some among you are leading an undisciplined life, doing no work at all, but acting like busybodies" (2 Thess. 3:10–11).

Prayer

Father God, please guide me in how I see success and how to help myself, my household, and others. Let me not be confused by the material world but may my trust, hope, and love be rooted in You. In Jesus name I pray. Amen.

Day 19

Correcting Oppression

Over the years there have been many great civil right activists who have stood up against the weight of oppression; some of them have been Christian, and some of them not. However, I would argue that the greatest activist known to mankind is God Himself. When it comes to justice, oppression, and speaking up He is loudly doing so for all of humanity.

> ¹⁷ *"Learn to do good; seek justice, correct oppression; bring justice to the fatherless, plead the widow's cause." (Isa. 1:17)*

For many years God has raised up some of the greatest activists and given them a moral compass and godly understanding to help untangle and to help correct the mistreatment that can result from oppression. You see, God always has a person to help correct oppression in the face of opposition. Although oppression is wrong, it is a reality that happens in every generation, and those who don't learn to help correct oppression, aren't really in the fight against it. We are all created for such a cause and purpose, but those who think that getting saved and going to church is the be-all and end-all of Christianity are horribly mistaking what the Christian life is all about. God never shares His word with us for plain observation but for clear participation. Since it is possible for all of us to be in participation of God's will, then it is disobedience when we are not. For some, it is uncomfortable or an inconvenience, but being a member of God's household includes disciplines and results. Being a part of the family of God means that you sometimes will have relatives that are lazy, rude and growing in different maturity stages. However, the thing about being in a household is that somethings responsibilities become shared and the same holds true for the household of God.

> **8 "But if anyone does not provide for his relatives, and especially for members of his household, he has denied the faith and is worse than an unbeliever." (1 Tim. 5:8)**

For believers in the household of God, it can be rough sometimes to get along with each other, but there is always something to offer to each other. Everyone is growing at a different pace, but God helps to bring the balance needed through His word. Many of us have different gifts to help edify each other but we are all to be subject to the word of God. Some brothers and sisters in the household of God offer a word of encouragement, mentorship while others pray fervently, evangelize and etc.. However, it is important that all of God's household is in participation and staying consistent for real change. We all may be feeling oppressed from time to time, but we also have a responsibility to get stronger and to help participate in the will/plan of God. In fact, none of us are excused. Even if some of our brothers and sisters work in privileged positions, the responsibility to God does not change. No matter what our position or status is in life, we are not excused from doing things Gods way. You can be a mom, dad, co-worker, spouse or whatever you are but your responsibility to God does not change. The bottom line is that if you are a Christian, then you have a responsibility. Unfortunately, one of the responsibilities that many lack in is in the responsibility to seek justice, and to correct oppression. The problem with this is that some people don't know how to fully define Gods plan of justice or know how to fully deal with oppression. Our approach in this topic is very important as well as actually getting involved with it. Regardless of how we feel about it, we are to help proclaim Gods truth in such matters. When we define things Gods way we can help correct many world issues and help to bring deliverance to the captives.

18 "The Spirit of the Lord is upon me, because he has anointed me to proclaim good news to

*the poor. He has sent me to proclaim liberty
to the captives and recovering of sight to the
blind, to set at liberty those who are oppressed,
19 to proclaim the year of the Lord's favor"
(Luke 4:18–19).*

Undoubtedly, if Christians step up and do their part, the world would be a much better place. After all, we shouldn't be called Christians if we can't do the things of Christ and live up to the identity of what God has given to us.

*20 "Therefore, we are ambassadors for Christ,
God making his appeal through us. We implore
you on behalf of Christ, be reconciled to God."
(2 Cor. 5:20)*

Reflection

Did you know that you have a responsibility to learn to do good, seek justice, and correct oppression? In what ways do you think that you can do that? Today, I want to encourage you to consider the places where you see the most oppression happening and to help bring a change either through influence, politically or through a non-profit that is already involved in it. Pray on it, and ask God to open doors.

Scripture

9 "The Lord is a refuge for the oppressed, a stronghold in times of trouble." (Ps. 9:9, NIV)

Prayer

Father God may my hands be found in helping others and helping others discover freedom in Christ Jesus. Cause my heart to want to get involved in the right things, and help my feet to walk on the right path. Heal me from any oppression that I may be free to proclaim You in boldness. Strengthen me toDay that I might not stumble. In Jesus name I pray. Amen.

Day 20

Are You Satisfied, Content, or Happy?

Did you know that being satisfied, content, or happy is a heart condition that reveals a lot about who we are or what state of mind that we are in? These words have a lot in common and are direct results of events or emotions to how we feel in life. Most importantly, the pursuit of these words are significant because they originate from God. God desires these words to be the reality of His people and their relationship to Him. God understands that when a person is satisfied, content, or happy that they are blessed and can help bless others. Becoming satisfied, content, or happy boil down to a heart condition.

Proverbs 15:13

A glad heart makes a cheerful face, but by sorrow of heart the spirit is crushed.

A lot of times we can find ourselves searching for things in life that will help make us satisfied, content, or happy because when we are, we are often friendlier, more relaxed, and more approachable. When being satisfied, content, or happy we are less affected by the problems around us and can deal with situations with a more welcoming personality. The truth is that sometimes a person's body language or attitude speak louder than their words. If a tree is recognized by its fruits, then what would make us any different? We are known by our attitude and body language, so when we display our happiness in God, then God is made known to others. It is important to note that our witness comes from the core of who we are, not entirely by the chores of what we do.

A satisfied, content, or happy person in God understands that God is the prize and treasure of life. To have a personal relationship with God is to understand true treasure. The presence of God is true treasure, and once you have experienced it wholeheartedly, you will know the medicine of it. Outside of God all other pursuits are rubbish.

Proverbs 17:22

"A joyful heart is good medicine, but a crushed spirit dries up the bones."

If you didn't know, God did not create you to have Him as second best in your life but as the prize of your life. However, the busyness of this world would have us think differently. It would pressure us to prioritize God as lesser, but to do so is to die spiritually and to lose the real treasure of life. Christians must learn to get the roots of satisfaction and happiness deeper into the presence of God and His fellowship. When we learn to deepen our relationship with God, the more satisfied, content, and happier we will be.

Reflection

Did you know that your true treasure in life should be God Himself? When you truly discover God, true happiness will come. ToDay ask God for a greater desire and relationship with Him.

Prayer

Father God please help me prioritize better of what's really important in life. May my heart beat after you and may I see you as the true treasure of life so that my heart would be content in you and not in the things that rust and fade away. In Jesus name I pray, Amen.

Day 21

Preach

Mark 16:15

*15 "And He said to them, "Go into all the world
and preach the gospel to every creature."*

D o you know what God means when he talks
about preaching? He means to publish and to
proclaim His truth. This does not mean that we are to
preach our own gospel, agenda, or definition of God
but His agenda and truth. Preaching is not for making
friends, persuading people, or for accumulating
wealth. Preaching is for the health of the people, the
repentance of the lost, and for the counsel of the hurt.
When proclaiming or publishing the word of God, we
must preach for health, not manipulation. God's word
is not to make puppets out of vulnerable people but to
make champions and warriors out of them. The truth
is that we are all like walking billboards and what we
say, proclaim, and live counts. When God's word is not
being proclaimed in difficult times, the truth becomes
muzzled, and disasters begin. Therefore, we should

preach in good health to bring health. In sharing the gospel, we are to never be biased or preach with biased motives. When preaching to someone, it doesn't matter if they have money or if they are homeless because the word of God does not change. Sometimes a preacher must step down if he or she has fallen while in leadership. If he or she wishes to be restored, then the elders and leadership of that community must pray, forgive, and agree about the readiness and position of that individual. Ultimately it is God who should be governing through people when they preach and especially through leadership, but the reality is that this isn't always the case. Some people preach out of a selfish agenda but for them God will deal with in the proper time. Ultimately, we all have a shared responsibility to live out what applies to us from what we hear and understand from God. In preaching to others, we should speak truthfully, examine ourselves and consider our approach. We should walk what we preach and if we mess up then we need to repent. We must remember that preaching is tied into what we say but seen by how we live.

² "Preach the word; be prepared in season and out of season; correct, rebuke and encourage— with great patience and careful instruction. ³ For the time will come when people will not put up with sound doctrine. Instead, to suit their own desires, they will gather around them a great

***number of teachers to say what their itching
ears want to hear" (2 Tim. 4:2–3, NIV).***

Reflection

Did you know that as a Christian you have a shared responsibility to preach the word of God? Did you know that you don't have to be a pastor to preach the word of God? We are ambassadors for God, and shyness should never hold us back from respectfully proclaiming the word of God. You and I can bring awareness of God's word, and with the right motive you we will see and help to bring change. I encourage you toDay to talk with someone about the Gospel when the opportunity arises.

Prayer

Father please, God, help me to love like You and to proclaim what You would have me proclaim. May my motives and heart be right, and with Your help may I have the energy and courage to walk in the identity You have called me to. In Jesus name, I pray. Amen.

Scripture

Romans 10:14

"How then will they call on him in whom they have not believed? And how are they to believe in him of whom they have never heard? And how are they to hear without someone preaching?"

Day 22

Convictions

H ave you ever felt like God was talking to you through your inner conviction? When God speaks to you through convictions, it is to show you something important. In the courtroom people get convicted for crimes they have committed. In other situations, people simply get convicted in their heart before or after making choices. In either case God speaks through conviction no matter if a person is a Christian or an atheist. One thing that a conviction does is puts a person in the spotlight before God. Convictions are personal because God is personal. God likes to deal with His people on a personal level because God wants a personal relationship with His creation.

"And when he comes, he will convict the world concerning sin and righteousness and judgment" *(John 16:8).*

Therefore, if you want to be a Holy Spirit kind of person then let God lead you and use the push of personal convictions. You may look or feel crazy when convictions put you in the spotlight, but when you do what's right, you will grow in your sensitivity and relationship to God. Following God through His leading is called obedience. God is a rewarder of obedience. Your reward may be peace of mind, monetary gain, wisdom, or whatever God so chooses, but if it comes from the hand of God, it is from the throne of God. The work of how God leads us and reveals things to us through conviction is a beautiful thing. We must not silence God by ignoring heart felt convictions but embrace Him according to His word when heart felt convictions come.

Reflection

Do you have heart felt convictions about God speaking to you or convictions about Him wanting to lead you somewhere? If so, I encourage you to follow Him. God will never mislead you, but sometimes your thinking will. Therefore, pray, confirm through scripture, and live like God wants you to.

Prayer

Father God, thank you for wanting a personal relationship with me. May I honor You when You talk to me and may my feet follow where You lead. Thank you for your guidance through

Your word and the work of the Holy Spirit. This I pray in Jesus name. Amen!

Scripture

John 14:26

"But the Helper, the Holy Spirit, whom the Father will send in my name, he will teach you all things and bring to your remembrance all that I have said to you."

Day 23

It's All Important

Could you imagine if certain foods were missing important ingredients? For example: French fries without ketch-up, steak without seasoning, cereal without milk, burritos without hot sauce, and so on and so forth? Wouldn't you agree that the quality would be affected? In like manner, the quality of a Christian's life isn't as great as it could be when he or she is halfheartedly walking in faith. The biblical principle is that we should be a people that puts more care into how we live and what we do. Our world is better when we care and treat it with importance. The consequences of not caring can cause trouble. Just imagine what it might look like if a husband constantly told his wife that what she thought wasn't important or if an employee didn't think that telling his or her supervisor why he or she was constantly late was important? How about if a doctor didn't think it was important to ask questions or to wear gloves during procedures? How about if a parent didn't care to discipline their kid? Again, how we treat everyday life is important. Often many people are more concerned about their physical life rather than their spiritual life, but this should not be the case. Our physical life is short compared to eternity. In fact, what you do as a Christian is top priority. Your prayer life is important, being joyful is important, fellowship is important, worshiping is important, kindness is important, serving is important, reading your Bible is important, loving others is important, and so on and so forth. All ingredients matter and should not be treated just as a grain of salt. After all, even salt is a small thing, but it still brings so much flavor into the world. When we begin to despise the small stuff, we invite trouble into our land and homes.

Song of Solomon 2:15

15 *"Catch the foxes for us, the little foxes that spoil the vineyards, for our vineyards are in blossom."*

We must catch and put in control those small things that can bring us trouble. We are at our best when we care about and do what's right.

Reflection

What do you consider to be important? Today, I want to encourage you to pay attention to the people around you and to consider how important each one of us is important to God. Allow God to minister to you and to teach you to care and pray better by what God reveals to you.

Prayer

Father, please help me treat the people in my life and the responsibilities that come my way with more importance. Help me to be intentional and therefore a light to those around me. May I live balanced and well-rounded for Your glory and honor. In Jesus name I pray. Amen.

Scripture

James 3:5

[5] "So also the tongue is a small member, yet it boasts of great things.
How great a forest is set ablaze by such a small fire!"

Day 24

Fix Your Focus

While one Day sitting at my mother's home, I looked up and saw that she had an engraved wooden decoration hanging from her wall in which read

"Fixing our eyes on Jesus, the author and perfecter of faith, who for the joy set before Him endured the cross, despising the shame, and has sat down at the right hand of the throne of God" (Heb. 12:2).

In that moment God had reminded me that if I would do better in fixing my focus on Him that He would fix my problems to come, either by guiding me or by complete intervention. Sometimes as Christians we forget that the battle belongs to the Lord and that fixing our focus belongs to us. In like manner, the same principle could be said about repentance and forgiveness: repentance belongs to us and forgiveness is what is given to us by God. When we fix our focus on God, we participate in our victory. The more we concentrate on God, the clearer things become. Too many times we are distracted and detoured by social media, work problems, home life issues, or whatever the case may be. However, if we don't take control of our wandering eyes, our eyes will keep on pursing more consuming issues.

Proverbs 27:20

"Hell and Destruction are never full;
So the eyes of man are never satisfied."

We must take charge of what we entertain and what we focus on. Our focus, and thought life are priorities to take care of. Many people only want to focus on God while in a mess but forget that being in sync with God prior to a mess can help prevent a mess or better handle a mess. For this reason, prevention is cure for some of life's greatest issues.

Reflection

Do you look to God when you have a problem? Do you have Scripture that can help bring you encouragement when needed? Today, choose to fix your focus on God.

Scripture

"In all your ways acknowledge him, and he will make straight your paths" (Prov. 3:6).

God's Plan

H ave you ever heard someone misuse or take out of context what the plan of God is for you? Well, you're not the only one, and sometimes people do make the mistake of talking out of turn. Every now and again you may find someone speaking out of turn because sometimes they only know in part because they only see in part.

9 "For we know in part and we prophesy in part,
10 but when completeness comes, what is in
part disappear." (1 Cor. 13:9–10).

This is true for any of us. God may let us see a portion of something, and we may feel like we have seen it all, but I promise that we don't know as much as we may think we do. God's ways are far greater than ours.

8 "For my thoughts are not your thoughts,
neither are your ways my ways," declares

> **the Lord. 9 "As the heavens are higher than the earth, so are my ways higher than your ways and my thoughts than your thoughts. (Isa. 55:8–9).**

Often times when Christians talk about the plan of God they are referring to God having an overall purpose or agenda. When speaking about the plan of God, it should be understood that God does have a plan for everyone, but a plan is just a plan, just like a map is just a map. God can share His plan with us but it doesn't mean that we are going to follow it. Think of Moses, who knew about the promised land but failed to get there himself. In other words, the plan of God is like a map for success, not necessarily the legwork needed. Too often when people rebel, they say things like, "It's part of God's plan," but in thinking of scripture, is it really? Although repentance is a part of God's redemption plan, sinning isn't Gods desire for us. As believers we are warned not to sin, so why would God tell us any different? The plan of God is to get us to a better place, not to lead us to a mess.

> **11 "For I know the plans I have for you, declares the Lord, plans for welfare[a] and not for evil, to give you a future and a hope" (Jer. 29:11).**

Yes, God has a plan for us but we must be able to follow His plan for us as individuals first and then as a body of believers. The plan of God is our best road map for an abundant life.

Reflection

Do you have a plan for your life? Do you know that God has a plan for you and that if you sincerely seek Him and ask Him sincerely for guidance that He will help you? You may think school, sports, or something else has something great to offer you but a part from the Lord all human plans will one Day come to an end. ToDay ask God for the guidance you need and follow where He will lead.

Scripture

21 "Many are the plans in the mind of a man,
but it is the purpose of the Lord that will stand."
(Prov. 19:21)

Prayer

Father God, thank you for having a plan for my life. I admit that sometimes I don't make the right plans in life, but with Your help and guidance, I can succeed. Help me toDay In Jesus name I pray. Amen.

From a Pastor`s Prospective

Living on Purpose, with a Purpose

by
Dr. Philip W. Calvert

Life happens. It happens every day. Every Day that you're alive, life happens. You don't need to think about it or plan for it. This is a valuable lesson we all learn—life will happen whether you want it to, ask for it, try to control it, or try to avoid it. Life happens. But, one day, it will all come to an end. Whatever that looks like personally for you, it is another valuable lesson: the final life happens, happens, and life itself comes to an end.

Since life happens for everyone, the challenge for all of us is to live in such a way that we can look back and honestly say that it was a life well-lived and that all of the life happens moments were worth it. The question is, how can we get to that moment, arguably the most poignant moment in a person's life, that moment when the dash between our date of birth and death becomes more real than it ever has been before—that moment when the final moment in that dash will be etched in stone and, from the vantage point of that moment looking back, we are able to say that it was an amazing journey!

You can read every book on happiness, success, and living an overcoming and victorious life that has ever been written, and all of those printed words boil down to one simple truth: the people who achieved their goals, lived joyfully, and could honestly smile when they drew their last breath were the people who lived on purpose. While life was happening around them and to them, they made every effort and took frequent risks, to not just navigate the choppy waters of life but to chart an exciting and well-defined course across those deep waters. Things happened to them, they made the most of those moments, and then they made things happen.

This is not about being an egomaniac or seeking wealth, for many people who lived life to the fullest disavowed the self and silver. Rather, what is in focus is the precious few who lived for something each Day that would survive that day—something greater than themselves that endured beyond a one-hour memorial service followed by a thirty-minute pot-luck luncheon.

And, of all the people who truly have something greater, much greater, to live for, is it not the follower of Jesus Christ? After all, we belong to Him and His eternal kingdom! When we give ourselves over to the God who made us, we truly become what He created us to be. In so doing we become far more than we could even imagine wanting to be: we become what He created us to be! How do we do that? How do we live that kind of life? The answer is simple, but the doing is difficult: we must allow God to have His way with us! Because He is our Creator, He knows exactly what kind of life He created for us, and what kind of life will bring comforting joy at the end of that life.

It is by God's grace that you were created, that you live, and that you have purpose. In living in full view of that grace, that unmerited favor, we truly become! In Second Timothy 1:9 we see that idea expressed beautifully. God saved us according to His grace and purpose through Jesus Christ, who is God the Son.

Despite our many mistakes and regardless of the family into which we were born, as a child of God we experience the grace of our loving heavenly Father every day. It is by that grace that you have a purpose for which to live!

Whatever you have done, wherever you have been, and whatever has been done to you, God has redeemed you with a purpose!

Because we were made by God our lives will be full of frustration and regret until we understand we were made for God. God's calling is about His plan for your life. Ephesians 2:10 gives us a great deal of guidance with regard to living on purposes. It reminds us that we were created by God and that in and through Jesus we have been created to do good works. That is great news!

On top of that, we are also reminded that God Himself prepared the work of our life ahead of time. That glorious thought is so wonderfully powerful! When we live for God the Father through His Son, Jesus, we know we are living a life of eternal purpose! We are made for a purpose, which God prepared in advance. We're God's creation. Ponder that reality for a moment. You are God's workmanship created in Christ Jesus to do good works. You were created to make a contribution with your life.

God gives us a purpose for His kingdom. This is a purpose that is far greater and far larger than our own life! However, to live for God's purpose, we must pursue His plans! You cannot fulfill God's purpose for your life while focusing on your own plans. Are you saved by the blood of Christ? Are you a child of God? I've got great news for you: God does not un-adopt His children! Even when Christians make mistakes and surrender the current shape of their call (such as when Christians fall into sin), God still has a call on their lives. He has a call on your life even if you have fallen into sin. If that is you today, don't give up! Confess those sins to the Lord, turn from those sins from now on, and live your life with purpose each day! That should be great news!

There is more great news. Whatever God calls you to do He's going to empower you to accomplish. He's going to provision you. He's going to undergird you. Your call to live His purpose is a walk of a lifetime. It's not a single step. Step out on faith. First Thessalonians 5:24 encourages us by saying that God called you and He is faithful to accomplish His plans.

That word faithful is the word I want to draw our hearts to as we draw this brief devotional to a close. There is another characteristic of joyful, productive, victorious people that is worth mentioning. Those who overcome are people who are faithful to something. Whether it is a business, a corporation, a nonprofit, an athletic career, or a ministry, people who joyfully succeed are people who steadfastly and faithfully live their lives in pursuit of some singular goal. For Christians, our focus is Christ! To be a follower of God means that we are passionate about following His Son! It means that we are focused on the end goal, which is God's eternal kingdom!

To live on purpose is to know that God created you, that He created you for something, that He knows what you need to accomplish His plans for your life, that He will provide a way, and that He expects you to devote your life with singular passion on a singular focus, which is His kingdom! That is what we call living the joy of our salvation.

Are you living on purpose? I pray that you are!

Day 26

God's Grace

Have you ever considered how unfair the grace of God can make others feel? If the truth be told, sometimes we don't want to give grace to others because we don't fully understand it or agree with it. However, grace is a huge part of God's character and a huge benefit for everyone. In fact, if there was no grace, then we would have pure law without any mercy and that is scary. Without grace there is a great separation between us and God. Grace isn't just a name, an appearance, or a gesture; it is a part of who God is (His character). When speaking about the grace of God, it means "unmerited favor." In fact, the grace of God is something that we don't deserve but is something that God extends to us. To get grace from God is very humbling. In God's grace, we get a lot of things that we don't deserve. For starters, He gave us a beautiful world to look after, but in return we have added pollution to it. He gives us the ability to have kids, but in return we allow abortions to happen and participate in irresponsible parenting. However, in all of our messy actions, God still offers to give us eternal life through faith and repentance instead of letting us sleep in the bed that we often make.

"Let us then with confidence draw near to the throne of grace, that we may receive mercy and find grace to help in time of need" (Heb. 4:16).

On the contrary, many people still oppose and undermine the grace of God with their pride, self-accomplishments, and an egotistic independence. Unfortunately for them, God won't tolerate it forever. There will be a Day of judgment and separation for how we live.

6 "But he gives more grace. Therefore it says, "God opposes the proud but gives grace to the humble." 7 Submit yourselves therefore to God. Resist the devil, and he will flee from you." (James 4:6–7)

Although Grace is great to have, we as individuals have to be mindful that God's grace is extended through our acceptance of Him.

8 "For by grace you have been saved through faith. And this is not your own doing; it is the gift of God, 9 not a result of works, so that no one may boast." (Eph. 2:8–9)

What Jesus Christ did for us on the cross was an act of love, grace, and mercy. We don't deserve it, but He loves us enough to offer it to us. As our faith stands with Him, His grace stands with us. By setting aside conflict and all other issues or hang-ups, our choice of looking to God can help fix current circumstances. Let us not misguide or take for granted the grace that has been shared with us.

Reflection

Did you know that God's grace is often extended in your acceptance of His plan for you? As you think of grace today, think of ways that you can share it in the remembrance of the cross. Remember that sometimes you have to give grace to others because God gave you grace when others wouldn't have.

Scripture

18 "But grow in the grace and knowledge of our Lord and Savior Jesus Christ. To him be the glory both now and to the Day of eternity. Amen."
(2 Pet. 3:18)

Prayer

(Pray this by yourself or out loud with your group)

Father God, I accept what You did for me on the cross through your son Jesus Christ. Please forgive me of my sins and help me to follow You. I accept You into my life as Lord and Savior. Please guide me toDay and in this very hour with not only my words but with Your help so I can stand with You. Make me committed and serious with a new heart.

In Jesus name I pray. Amen.

Day 27

Approach

D id you know that your approach in life can affect your outcome to some of life's most challenging problems? Better yet, have you ever made someone mad at you by approaching them with a wrong attitude or tone of voice? Believe it or not, some people are sensitive to how you approach them or handle yourself. The Bible is clear that it matters how we carry ourselves.

> *13 "Let us behave decently, as in the daytime, not in carousing and drunkenness, not in sexual immorality and debauchery, not in dissension and jealousy. 14 Rather, clothe yourselves with the Lord Jesus Christ, and do not think about how to gratify the desires of the flesh."*
> *(Rom. 13:13–14)*

Although a person may have the identity of being a Christian, he or she is still subject to the consequence of a bad approach. Just like a zookeeper wouldn't want to approach the animals of the zoo in a wrong way, the same is true for Christians who are not only dealing with their own growth but also the issues of others. For example, think of the following scripture:

> ***"A soft answer turns away wrath, but a harsh word stirs up anger" (Prov. 15:1).***

Could you imagine how horrible things could get if we approached others who were already angry, in depression, panicked, or whatever the case may be with the wrong attitude? In life God knows that people have trigger issues and self-control problems. Therefore, to approach others outside of love is to deal with them at the risk of harm. In the counsel of the Bible, God speaks to us about our choice of conduct because the right approach helps to make a better outcome.

Reflection

Did you know that the approach of love will help build a successful future? When you approach others with the true definition of love, you harvest real success. With the right approach in life, you will discover a better world and atmosphere.

Prayer

Lord God may my approach be seasoned with salt and a beacon of light for others. Help me to discover the love that You want me to share with others that I might help change the atmosphere around me. May Your approach be the behavior of my life. In Jesus name I pray. Amen.

Scripture

15 "Look carefully then how you walk, not as unwise but as wise, 16 making the best use of the time, because the days are evil. 17 Therefore do not be foolish, but understand what the will of the Lord is" (Eph. 5:15–17).

Struggle

D id you know that sometimes it's good to have a little bit of struggle in life? Contrary to the belief that life is always going to be pleasant, the Bible says different.

James 1:2–3

2 "Count it all joy, my brothers, when you meet trials of various kinds, 3 for you know that the testing of your faith produces steadfastness."

It is clear that we will have hard days to live through. Some of our hardships will come from our own actions, and some will come from the actions of others. In either case we know that hardships are coming. When the Bible talks about putting on the armor of God (Eph. 6:10–18) or us fighting the good fight of faith (1 Tim. 6:12) it is because God doesn't want us to be blindsided or unprepared when the fight comes to us. God wants you and I to be successful in life and sometimes the allowance of a struggle, rejection, and pain is the school of character that is needed. In Western Christianity the church is often centered around a gospel that makes you feel good versus a gospel that brings you character. Yes, it is true that God wants you to be blessed, and in Christ Jesus you are. You may not feel blessed in your financial life, but what anyone of us feels like dose not necessarily determine who we are in Christ Jesus. Our first concern should be our spiritual life, not our financial situation. You see, the scriptures you choose to read will change your mindset, but when you lean on the whole counsel of God, it will change your lifestyle. This is why preachers and bible teachers constantly invest their life in scripture because life itself can be found in the living word of God.

Reflection

Did you know that struggle can help you grow? Today, if you are dealing with hardships, just remember that God Loves you and wants you to lean on Him. Life may bring you challenges, but God has not left you empty-handed. Get focused on God, stay focused on God, and win. In Christ Jesus you have the victory!

Prayer

Father God, teach me Your ways. Give me a true desire for You. I don't want to define success by the standards of this world but by the truth of Your word. Minister to me toDay that I may stand awakened and afresh. In Jesus name I pray. Amen!

Scripture

Romans 8:18

18 "For I consider that the sufferings of this present time are not worth comparing with the glory that is to be revealed to us."

Day 29

Messy Emotions

H ave you ever had emotions get the best out of you? Sometimes our emotions are ugly and damaging to our health, relationships, and our testimony. We are not as effective when we let emotions counsel us. Honestly, only God should be our great counselor, and when we let emotions counsel us, we will often discover that someone is affected by it. When we are pushed back and forth by emotions, it says something about our stability and theology in God.

Ephesians 4:13–15

13 "until we all reach unity in the faith and in the knowledge of the Son of God and become mature, attaining to the whole measure of the fullness of Christ.

14 Then we will no longer be infants, tossed back and forth by the waves, and blown here and there by every wind of teaching and by the cunning and craftiness of people in their deceitful scheming. 15 Instead, speaking the

truth in love, we will grow to become in every respect the mature body of him who is the head, that is, Christ"

I have learned that when I am easily panicked, angered, depressed, or something else, that I am not as stable as I should be. Our stability should not depend on emotions that can fail us but on scripture that leads us to character. Yes, it is true, we all have emotions, and we all need to deal with our emotions appropriately. How we feel often leads us to what we do, but as Christians we must be led by what God says. Take the example of unforgiveness when two people are in conflict and fight. Instead of fighting in anger, they really should be concerned about fixing what is needed and reconciling. Real maturity will speak for itself. God cares about how we respond to others in life because how we respond reflects what is inside of us. On the cross Jesus could have responded in revenge to the insults against Him, but He didn't, and remained in love. Honest maturity reflects through character but undisciplined emotions can make scars.

Reflection

Have you been reacting in emotions lately? Today, I want to encourage you to better yourself when you feel like being immature in any situation that may come your way. Ask God to help you and to correct your heart and lips as necessary.

Prayer

Father God, I pray against the desires of my ungodly emotions and for Your character in my life. Let me not be foolish in my own ways but healthy in Your ways. If I have a chemical imbalance, then heal me and use me. I thank You for caring and wanting the best for my life. I ask for Your help toDay in Jesus name. Amen!

Scripture

Romans 12:2

² "Do not be conformed to this world, but be transformed by the renewal of your mind, that by testing you may discern what is the will of God, what is good and acceptable and perfect."

Can You Be Happy with Less?

The pursuit of happiness has always been like an unending race for many people. Happiness is something that God wants us to have because in happiness there isn't much complaining or fighting but contentment. However, the pursuit of happiness and the reason for happiness is where many problems begin. For example, being happy in sin is the wrong place to be. In fact, being happy in your sin is no reason to live in your sin. Even though God wants you to have the experience of happiness, He does not want you to be happy through the decay of sin or the pursuit of it. To be happy in the pursuit of sin is to already be poisoned by sin. A desire for the pleasure of happiness through the means of sin will only bring the consequences of sin.

¹⁴ "But each person is tempted when he is lured and enticed by his own desire. ¹⁵ Then desire when it has conceived gives birth to sin, and

sin when it is fully grown brings forth death."
(James 1:14–15)

The truth is that God isn't interested in our joy for this world as much as He is interested in our preparation for eternity. Our prep work for eternity has a lot to do with our desire for Jesus Christ here and now. What God has done for us is something that we have to accept and understand on a personal level. You see, God wants a relationship with us, not just an encounter. Although many Christians confess Jesus Christ as Lord and Savior, they will often find themselves challenged by what they claim to be true and confess. This is where the real test begins. When a man or a woman is tested by how content he or she can be with just having a relationship with God is where real growth begins.

11 "Not that I am speaking of being in need, for
I have learned in whatever situation I am to
be content. 12 I know how to be brought low,
and I know how to abound. In any and every
circumstance, I have learned the secret of facing
plenty and hunger, abundance and need. 13 I can
do all things through him who strengthens me.
(Phil. 4:11–13, ESV)

5 "Keep your life free from love of money, and
be content with what you have, for he has
said, "I will never leave you nor forsake you.""
(Heb. 13:5)

Being content in God is rewarding in itself.

Reflection

Today, in this devotion, consider what really makes you happy. Ask yourself what hinders you from chasing after a deeper relationship with God and pray on it. Ask yourself why God created you and whether you can truly be happy with less stuff in this life and more of Him.

Day 31

Judging

W hen you think about "judging" what do you think about—or perhaps who do you think about? Often the topic of judging stirs up a lot of emotions and turmoil for various reasons, but the reality is that judging others happens whether we like it or not. In this devotion I will point out a few things for consideration, but the overall goal is to remind the Christian of a few necessary principles.

In terms of judging others or being judged by others, some people feel like they can't be judged by certain people because certain people are hypocritical or unfit to tell them anything. Other times people don't want to hear about "judging" because of their own guilty conscience. However, this topic for the Christian isn't a topic to run from or to be frightened of. Everyone is guilty of somethin (*Rom. 3:23*), and if they weren't, then they wouldn't need forgiveness from Jesus. If we didn't need forgiveness, we could basically walk right into heaven, but that's not how it works. Some people may feel like they are good people, but the

Bible reminds us that we all have sinned *(Rom. 3:23)* and if you don't believe what that verse says then read the Ten Commandments (*Exod. 20*) and ask yourself which one of those commandments have you broken? For example, if you have stolen something, then you are guilty of theft; if you have dishonored your parents, then you are guilty of not honoring them. No matter how big or small you think your sin is, it is still sin and requires judgment because God is just.

The point is that If you do something wrong, then you are wrong. Even if you don't get caught for something you did recently or in the past, it doesn't matter. God will enforce justice, and none of us are excused from it but are responsible to how we respond.

As Christians when we are guilty of something then we must deal with it in a Christlike manner, and if we are not guilty, then we must keep walking in the truth. Even if someone has something bad to say about you and decides to judge you on something you did or something they heard about, then you shouldn't take offense. Instead be wise in defusing a potential fight by apologizing for any misunderstanding or wrongdoing and then continue on with your day. For the most part you don't owe anyone anything accept the debt of love.

Romans 13:8

8 "Owe no man any thing, but to love one another: for he that loveth another hath fulfilled the law."

If people can't accept who you are, then you shouldn't try to force them to accept you. Your godly response is much more important than your entertainment for anyone or for you to be offended by anyone. When judgment comes your way, make peace if possible. The last thing that the church needs is more gossip and more offense because people don't know how to talk to each other but only about each other. Yes it's true that we need to have discernment in our life and to speak up on things that are unhealthy, but it is not our position to hold a grudge against others or to hang a life sentence against them. When you point something out to someone, make sure that it is God in you who is doing the speaking and not your flesh because then you invite judgment against yourself. Overall, if you become judged, then make sure it lines up with God's word and that you deal with it in a Christlike manner. On the other hand, if you are going to make a judgment then make sure it is from God's word and seek correction and a solution that restores, not a problem. Don't ever paint people out to be ugly when God has created them in His image.

Reflection

Did you know that people can sometimes be used by God to be your indicator to a solution or a reminder? How God helps us grow can sometimes feel strange to us but it is necessary. Being judged is sometimes a tool to help us grow. If you have something you been judged on lately, I want to encourage you to seek humbleness, correction, and love as needed. In doing things the right way, you will often discover peace within.

Prayer

Father God please help me to discern correctly so that I won't damage others. May I learn to use situations as a tool for my personal growth. In return, may my life be of health to others. Teach me how to help others find life and not condemnation. This I pray in Jesus name. Amen!

Scripture

John 7:24

24 "Do not judge by appearances, but judge with right judgment."

Relationship

D id you know that the kind of relationships you have with others will determine the openness and trust that you share with them? As human beings, we have different kinds of relationships with different people. Some relationships include friendship, acquaintanceships, being a neighbor, becoming an adopted family member, and so on and so forth. For each relationship there are different boundaries. For example, if you are a friend to someone, then you more than likely have the privilege to ask certain questions, confide in them, and to be more transparent with each other. The measure of the relationship between you and someone else is what really makes a difference in communication. In like manner, God too has a relationship with each one of us, but each relationship is fueled by proximity. The closer you walk and talk with God, the more you understand Him, and the more He shares with you.

14 "You are my friends if you do what I command. 15 I no longer call you servants, because a servant does not know his master's business. Instead, I have called you friends, for everything that I learned from my Father I have made known to you. 16 You did not choose me, but I chose you and appointed you so that you might go and bear fruit—fruit that will last— and so that whatever you ask in my name the Father will give you." (John 15:14–16)

One major point to understand is that you get to choose what you share with others depending on the relationship and closeness you have with them. As a friend with God He chooses to share important things with you. In the Bible God made sure to share things with his servants.

Genesis 18:17–18

17 "And the Lord said, "Shall I hide from Abraham what I am doing, 18 since Abraham shall surely become a great and mighty nation, and all the nations of the earth shall be blessed in him?"

Amos 3:7

7 "Surely the Lord God does nothing, Unless He reveals His secret to His servants the prophets."

If you didn't know, God is serious about relationships. Everything that God does for you is to help bring you into a right relationship with Him. When you have a right relationship with God, all other relationships can serve a healthier purpose. Having a friend in Jesus isn't like having an ordinary friendship because a friendship with Jesus is a friendship that involves heaven. The thing about having a personal relationship with God is that He is not just available as a friend but as a Father, a Counselor, an Advocate, and so much more. Sadly, some people will not become friends with God but become enemies of God.

4 "Adulterers and adulteresses! Do you not know that friendship with the world is enmity with God? Whoever therefore wants to be a friend of the world makes himself an enemy of God. (James 4:4)

Having a personal relationship with God is having a personal experience and encounter with God regularly. In like manner, the same goes for other kind of relationships, and this is the reason God doesn't want you to be involved in certain relationships with the world. If you want to share your heart and mind in wickedness, then don't expect God to join you or to bless you with what's contrary to Him. God will not approve of what keeps you from Him. God is very personal, and that is why sometimes He will not allow you to experience Him in certain places but in the privacy between you and Him. When you know how to walk and talk with God privately, you will better know how to walk, talk and trust Him more openly. Having an individual relationship with God first will guide you best. Becoming better husbands, wives, friends, leaders and more all start with you and God first.

Reflection

Did you know that having a right relationship with God can build greater relationships with others? More importantly, in the privacy of your time is where God communes with you best? God loves you and wants your undivided attention, not the back of your head or just an amen.

Scripture

3 "Do two walk together, unless they have agreed to meet? (Amos 3:3)

Prayer

Father God, please send the Holy Spirit to help me today. Help me to know Jesus Christ more personally that I may know how to grow in the best possible way. May I have a real and true relationship with You right here and right now. Grow me up. In Jesus name I pray. Amen!

Day 33

Health

D id you know that some people strive to be in good health for their image and some strive to get in good health to preserve their life? For many this topic is sensitive but needed. As a Christian your health is to glorify God.

1 Corinthians 6:19–20

19 "Or do you not know that your body is a temple of the Holy Spirit within you, whom you have from God? You are not your own, 20 for you were bought with a price. So glorify God in your body."

Our body is not for seduction, sale, or self-gratification but for God. In America we see people deal with self-image problems as well as problems of obesity and diabetes. Unfortunately, anytime the Bible becomes ignored in such matters, the consequences speak. God has made us in His image and cares that we take care of our health.

Genesis 1:27

[27] "So God created man in his own image, in the image of God he created him; male and female he created them."

When God made us, it was personal and intentional. Therefore, to ignore that God created you in His image is personal and intentional as well. Yes, the consequences of sin has affected us all, but we must do better to remember that the continuance of sin will destroy us. God cares when we promote selfishness in our body or gluttony from our appetites. To disrespect God's temple is to trespass against God.

As Christians in the Western culture, we are blessed in a supply of food, but we must be careful not to disrespect the hand who blesses us with such privilege. We need to be better stewards of our health and treat our bodies with the care of God in mind.

Reflection

Do you use your body for the honor of God? Do you have a problem with your weight? Today, I want to encourage you to fast from a food item for the next thirty days that you may be abusing. I also want to encourage you to be modest about your body not self-glorifying. In your fast ask God for His help and when tempted remind yourself to honor God.

Prayer

Thank you, God, for new challenges and chances to glorify you in my body. May I do well and live well in Jesus name, I pray. Amen!

Scripture

3 John 2

2 "Beloved, I pray that all may go well with you and that you may be in good health, as it goes well with your soul."

Day 34

Victory

love the idea of everyone having victory in life, but I don't always like the reality of how much victory can cost. I'm sure that God uses the word *victory* for many great reasons, but today I want to focus on a couple of points. When we think of the word victory, we can often picture the outcome and imagine a celebration, but how many times do we actually think about the fight in between? When God talks about victory, it's because there is a lot to consider. Yes, God wants us to experience the great things that come with victory but He does not want us to take the journey to victory for granted. There is ownership in earning a victory and a thankfulness for getting it. Victory for the Christian is to ultimately bring God praise, but victory for the unbeliever is often about self-glorification. Sometimes victory can be taken for granted when it shouldn't be. Some people even think that praying to God will grant them a free hand out to victory, but if the truth be told, God often gives a person the strength for victory and helps guide them to victory. God doesn't always just give us a bunch of free handouts to everything and anything. Obedience and grace has a lot to do with understanding that God is ultimately the source to true victory.

4 *"for the Lord your God is he who goes with you to fight for you against your enemies, to give you the victory.'"(Deut. 20:4)*

What people often mistake about God is that God offers opportunities, not necessarily free handouts. With God you have to learn to put in the work because nothing about Jesus dying on the cross for you was free to Him. For this reason there is a disrespect in rejecting what Jesus did for you on the cross and how much agony it cost God the Father. Real victory requires real effort, work and obedience. Victory is not just a church name or a catchy word but a serious accomplishment. You can talk or daydream about victory, but you can't have it until you are willing to get right with God. There is victory in Jesus, which is why there is rejoicing in heaven when people get saved. In your struggle to victory, remember Jesus.

Reflection

Have you been taking some victories in your life for granted? Are you in need of a victory today? Today, deeply and sincerely pray about it. God is in the business of victory; let Him tug at your heart to do what's needed.

Prayer

Father God, let me not take this life that You have given me for granted. Forgive me of my sins and guide me where I'm at right here and right now. Grant me a fresh start right here and right now, In Jesus name I ask and pray. Amen.

Scripture

"But thanks be to God, who gives us the victory through our Lord Jesus Christ." (1 Cor. 15:57)

Day 35

Parenting

Have you ever known someone who has been affected by their childhood? Sadly, there are plenty of statistics each year showing that neglect, abandonment, and abuse have profound impact on a person's life. Today, many absent parents exist for multiple reasons. Unfortunately, too many absent parents are imprisoned, on drugs, living for selfish reasons, and sometimes even in the busyness of work. If you think about it, the fact that children psychologists and counselors exist is the evidence of a lack of parenting in the land. By the method and standard in which a country will parent with, will either be pleasing to God or unpleasing. Parenting is a gift from God and we as parents will have to give account for how we raise the children that He gives to us.

Psalm 127:3

"Behold, children are a heritage from the Lord, the fruit of the womb a reward."

The word heritage and the word reward used in Psalm 127:3 is powerful. Having a child is a big responsibility. Parents are to train up their children in the way that they should go, not necessarily in the way that they want to go.

Proverbs 22:6

"Train up a child in the way he should go; even when he is old he will not depart from it."

The word *train* used in Proverbs 22:6 is a big word because it requires responsibility, not neglect. When the responsibility to raise a child becomes neglected, then the results begin to show. God expects us to teach our children and to model what's right. Kids don't need to be introduced to the evil in the world but to the goodness of God. When kids want to do wrong it is the responsibility of the guardian to redirect or discipline.

Proverbs 22:15

"Folly is bound up in the heart of a child, but the rod of discipline drives it far from him."

Proverbs 29:17

"Discipline your son, and he will give you rest; he will give delight to your heart."

Discipline is a God-given responsibility not to be abused. Sometimes love can be seen in the form of discipline, but in other times it is seen when a parent is present and providing care and guidance. If you are a parent or guardian, do not despise what God puts before you.

Reflection

Did you know that God cares about how a person or country raises up children? Children are a blessing from God, and if you are a parent or guardian, I want to encourage you to love and to look to God for guidance. Your responsibility is great! Not every child growing up gets to have a godly role model.

Prayer

Father, thank you for all that You do. Please help every parent and child come to the saving knowledge of Jesus Christ and to experience true joy in You. I pray for every child who has been affected by bad parenting and a victim to neglect: please meet them where they are and be their light in the dark. Teach us to do better as a country and as individuals. This I pray in Jesus name. Amen!

Scripture

Luke 18:16

"But Jesus called them to him, saying, "Let the children come to me, and do not hinder them, for to such belongs the kingdom of God."

Marriage From a Minister's Prospective

By
Ray & Kathy Land

Marriage is a visible demonstration to the world of Jesus's love for the church for the glory of God. Couples have a 100 percent chance of an amazing relationship when they follow God's guidance for marriage outlined in the Bible. We are to love each other, serve each other, and respect each other out of deference for Christ Jesus. God must be kept at the center of every relationship through fervent prayer, thanksgiving, and worship. We are to seek God's will for every decision, choice, and action in our marriages.

God brings every couple together for a specific kingdom purpose and assignment. Each couple is responsible to understand the unique purpose for their union and accomplish the mission God has given them. The vision for marriage can be unclear until they begin to walk together obediently in their purpose and step into their blessing. When a couple walks in purpose with passion and love, their blessings will chase after them and overflow into their lives.

Healthy marriages upset the enemy and the spiritual warfare attacks will escalate against them. It's important for couples to stand firm, worship God, and love each other with His unconditional *agape* love. They must be willing to fight for their marriage instead of fighting against each other. Once they understand source of the attacks against them, they can take full spiritual authority and claim victory over the enemy.

Strong marriages lead to strong families. Strong families lead to strong churches. Strong churches lead to strong communities. Strong communities lead to strong, cities, states, countries, and a strong kingdom of heaven on earth. Let's keep our marriages strong for the kingdom.

Ray & Kathy Land
Book Author: *5 Key Principles to Freedom from the Inside Out*

The "IF" Word

It wouldn't be forgiveness "IF" love
wasn't involved.

It wouldn't be hate "IF" anger wasn't involved.

It wouldn't be Christianity "IF" Christ
wasn't involved.

It wouldn't be victory "IF" fighting
wasn't involved.

Growing up I learned that we all have an "IF" to deal with. The word "IF" is a very conditional word and a very powerful one. Therefore, when dealing with this word or words like "IF," I am reminded that we are creatures of condition. Not only do we have a spiritual and physical condition to think about, but we also do things based on conditions. For example: "IF" we work, then we expect health insurance and expect to get paid under the terms and conditions of the job. By nature, we want to know what's in it for us. "IF" it sounds good and seems to work well, then we put our faith in it. Now don't get me wrong—this isn't a bad thing, depending on what's involved. Obviously if sin is involved and hurting others is involved, then don't participate in it. God is against evil. By God's very own nature He is for the good and health of a person's life because He is the source of life and the source of all good things that pertain to salvation. If physical or spiritual health is involved, then God is involved because God is in the business of bringing about good health and second chances. One way God does this is by giving all of us the ability to be skillful and responsive to what is needed, but it is up to us to participate in those things that produce the most good. The truth is that "IF" we want to be right with God, then we must come to understand the options that we have when God uses the "IF" word in our life.

31 "So Jesus said to the Jews who had believed him, "If you abide in my word, you are truly my disciples, 32 and you will know the truth, and the truth will set you free." (John 8:31–32)

When God uses the word "IF" in our life, He is helping to remind us of who we are and of the options that we have. Overall, "IF" any of us wants to truly please God, then our actions and maturity will show.

14 "If My people who are called by My name will humble themselves, and pray and seek My face,

and turn from their wicked ways, then I will hear from heaven, and will forgive their sin and heal their land." (2 Chron. 7:14)

The word "IF" can be a great heart checker and reflection for us that we shouldn't take lightly.

Reflection:

Today, what "IF" words are you dealing with? Are you stuck in between a hard decision? Have you asked yourself what will happen "IF" you do the right thing? Following God isn't easy but it is worth it because spiritual health is worth it. If you are in a tough situation, then I want to encourage you to do the right thing with God first by praying and lifting your petition to Him. After, I want to encourage you to do the right thing and to continue doing the right thing because giving up won't bring you the real victory needed. Always live for purpose, not for ego.

Scripture

5 Now therefore, if you will indeed obey My voice and keep My covenant, then you shall be a special treasure to Me above all people; for all the earth is Mine. 6 And you shall be to Me a kingdom of priests and a holy nation.' These are the words which you shall speak to the children of Israel."
(Exod. 19:5–6)

Prayer

Father God, I sometimes feel and hear that doing right is the right thing to do, but I sometimes have a wrong heart. Please reposition my heart and help me to live out my calling. I want to love You more and want to live for love that isn't fake. Make Yourself more real in me so I can make the right and necessary decisions needed. In Jesus name I pray. Amen!

Influence and Stumbling Blocks

Yes, it's true: for some people influence should be a crime. Well, from reading the Bible I would dare to agree that it is a crime of punishment. If you don't believe me, think about what happened in the garden when Satan tempted Eve (Gen. 3:1–4) and how disobedience came about. Later the Bible shows that after disobedience came about through Eve and Adam that judgment for humanity did as well. This judgment also included punishment for the serpent who was found as the influencer (Gen. 3:13–19). The word *influence* is a powerful word, and it deals with the development of a person's thinking and behavior. Although some people wouldn't want to be held responsible for their influence over certain matters, with God they aren't excused from when and how they participated through their influence. As Christians we are accountable for how we influence, guide, teach, and behave. Undoubtedly, influence has persuasion and a great sales pitch, but when it is used as a stumbling block of evil, it is sinful and harmful. At any time when influence helps to create or campaign for a negative development, it turns into a stumbling block for evil. The truth is, when people create stumbling blocks from wrongful desires, God is neither pleased nor glorified.

In such matters, God has a lot to say about the participation of influence, stumbling blocks and obstacles:

"Therefore let us stop passing judgment on one another. Instead, make up your mind not to put any stumbling block or obstacle in the way of a brother or sister." (Rom. 14:13)

And it will be said: "Build up, build up, prepare the road! Remove the obstacles out of the way of my people." (Isa. 57:14)

"Be careful, however, that the exercise of your rights does not become a stumbling block to the weak." (1 Cor. 8:9)

If we take this subject further, then remember what is said about those who teach and how they have a greater judgment upon themselves?

"Not many of you should become teachers, my brothers, for you know that we who teach will be judged with greater strictness." (James 3:1)

Becoming involved in a place of influence, means a lot of responsibility. Honestly, we should all be careful how we bring influence to our family members, community and what we share on social media. What we endorse or participate in is very important. If our influence is wrong then we need to repent.

Reflection

Have you ever been influenced to do something bad, or have you ever been the influencer of something bad? Did you know that God cares about how we are influenced and who we are influencing? Today, I want to encourage you to consider becoming more of an influencer of God by how you talk and by how you acknowledge Him. When given the opportunity help others, know the boundaries of good and evil. Share this devotion with someone and ask them what they think.

Prayer

Father God, may I not be formed by anyone's persuasion or cleverness but please help me to be transformed by Your truth alone. I only want to deal with the truth so that I am not found living a lie. There is freedom in your truth and hope for the world. Let me not be shaped by the influence of others but quickened to overcome any obstacle that comes my way. I have faith in you, please help me to do right and stay right. In Jesus name I pray. Amen.

Scripture

14 "I know and am persuaded in the Lord Jesus that nothing is unclean in itself, but it is unclean for anyone who thinks it unclean." (Rom. 14:14)

Day 38

Peace

Wouldn't it be nice to be at peace with God and to be at peace with others? You see, God's word is given in such a way to help us obtain peace and to maintain it. However not everyone is at peace with God or at peace with His word. Some people have no peace with God because they have found worldly rest in the cloaked dangers of sin. In other cases, some would rather go to war with God in the name of justice but in a definition that isn't defined by God. Others have found a resting place in the poison or sedation of drugs and alcohol, only to discover that there is no true peace in the consequences of their misbehavior. The truth is that many people aren't at peace with God because they are at war with Him. Often times there is a fight against God because people cherish the power of decisions rather than the choice of submission. Although peace is what God would like for us to experience, sometimes we would rather give Him a piece of our mind instead receiving the peace that He has to offer. Thankfully we are reminded to pursue peace because God knows what's most beneficial for us. Pursing peace doesn't always mean that our hardships will go away, but it does mean that we are on the right path of problem solving. Sometimes we have to war against our flesh to make peace with God. Ultimately, what we pursue is what will make a difference. If we become rooted in Christ then the peace of God will become rooted in us.

Reflection

Did you know peace is a good sign of health? In Romans 15:33 God is known as the God of peace, and with that statement alone, we can be certain to know that seeking after God is the right pursuit to heavenly peace. Today, ask God for this peace of the Bible and get closer to Him. God wants a strong and personal relationship with you.

Prayer

Father God, I would like some more of Your peace and happiness within my life. Please mature me in this peace of knowing You and may I in turn help inspire others to know You. Deepen this peace within my soul and bring it for the edification of my growth. Have Your way within my life. In Jesus name I pray. Amen!

Scriptures

[18] *"If possible, so far as it depends on you, live peaceably with all.*[19] *Beloved, never avenge yourselves, but leave it*[a] *to the wrath of God, for it is written, "Vengeance is mine, I will repay, says the Lord."* [20] *To the contrary, "if your enemy is hungry, feed him; if he is thirsty, give him something to drink; for by so doing you will heap burning coals on his head."* [21] *Do not be overcome by evil, but overcome evil with good.* (Rom. 12:18–21)

"You keep him in perfect peace whose mind is stayed on you, because he trusts in you" (Isa. 26:3).

"Strive for peace with everyone, and for the holiness without which no one will see the Lord" (Heb. 12:14).

Two Great Questions

There are two great questions asked in the Bible that I believe every believer should reflect on. In the first question that I want to mention is when Jesus asked His disciple Peter, "Who do you say that I am?" (Matt. 27:22) In the second question, a Roman ruler by the name of Pilate asked the people what he should do with Jesus who is called the Messiah during the time that Jesus was imprisoned, wrongly mistreated, and unjustly charged (*Matt. 27:22*). Now let's take a few seconds to reflect and personalize these two questions:

Question #1. Who do I say that Jesus is?

Question #2. What should I do with Jesus who is called the Messiah?

As Christians we have to give an account to the claims we make about Jesus. We are accountable to our study of Him, our time that we give Him, and how we identify Him. Although the identity of Jesus isn't dependent on our understanding of Him, it is obtainable through God's word and revelation to us. Once we have a God perspective of who Jesus is, then we must decide whether we are going to follow Him or not. Following Jesus is a choice, and that choice is a personal choice that we all have to make. We prioritize so many things in life, but once we are confronted by what the will of God is and by the convictions of the Spirit, then we are held accountable to do whatever is right and to make the right changes in our life. God loves us and helps us to develop through our reading of the Bible and through the conviction of His Spirit. However, it is important that we identify and respond to Him when we recognize Him reaching out to us. On the other hand, the devil would like to keep us busy and distracted but making time to know God better is an absolute way of life. Following Jesus is a journey and a journey that we must choose to follow.

Reflection

Today, have you identified who Jesus is? Are you okay with making more time to study and to prioritize how Jesus can be more involved in your everyday life? What will you do about the things you are learning through God's word, and when should you start applying the things you have learned?

Scripture

"What shall I do, then, with Jesus who is called the Messiah?" Pilate asked.

They all answered, "Crucify him!" (Matt. 27:22)

"But what about you?" he asked. "Who do you say I am?" (Matt. 16:15)

Prayer

Lord God, please help me to maximize my time with You. It is healthy for me to follow You, yet it is hard for me at certain times of my life. Therefore, please help me in my weakness that I may rise above the enemy's desire to devour me. May I do what's right in Your sight starting right here and right now. In Jesus name I pray. Amen!

Day 40

Why Expect?

Why expect good when choosing to live bad?

Why expect justice when choosing to
live unjustly?

Why expect money when refusing to work?

Why expect heaven when living devilishly?

Why expect trophies when refusing to practice?

Why expect respect when refusing to
give respect?

Why expect to be a leader when
refusing to serve?

Why expect change while not willing to change?

Why expect to learn by just daydreaming?

Why expect friendships when being unfriendly?

Why expect victory while unwilling to fight?

Why expect good health when constantly
eating horribly?

Why expect security when living risky?

Why expect much while giving so little?

Refection

Do you ever find yourself in any of the mentioned things above? If so, then why not work on fixing it today? First admit to God where you are messing up, and then ask Him for forgiveness and the help that you need. Second, start to be a doer and keep practicing, even if you fail and feel like giving up. God can see your efforts, and He wants you to talk with Him about your growth and where you need direction. Sometimes we don't like the answer that God gives us, but we can't expect to be at our best when we won't let Him lead us to our best.

Scripture

"But be doers of the word, and not hearers only, deceiving yourselves" (James 1:22).

Prayer

Father God, please help me to be more responsible in the things that I should be doing here on earth. Help me not to be expecting so much from others and You when I'm not willing to do my part. As I grow, continue to remind be in conviction, concern and in love where my priorities are. In Jesus name I pray. Amen.

Day 41

Anger and Temper Tantrums

H ave you ever had a temper tantrum as a kid or as an adult? In your opinion at what age is it okay to have a temper tantrum? Sometimes when we don't get what we want, we can get angry and ugly. People notice and can often see when we are angry. Even temper tantrums are noticeable because they are outbursts of frustration and a lack of controlled anger. Some tantrums are so severe that people go to jail over it, and some people cause physical damage because of it. Other tantrums create a drive to be passive aggressive and revengeful. Sadly, temper tantrums exist in our world, but more importantly, people throw tantrums with God. They don't like that God corrects them or doesn't give them things that they have prayed for. As a result, they turn their backs on Him. People do the same thing with churches: if they have disagreements, they'd rather get emotional about it and talk badly about the church or others without first addressing it properly. However, this is not a trait of godly character. Jesus didn't get off the cross because people rejected Him and spit on Him. Neither did Jesus throw a temper tantrum when Judas betrayed Him. Jesus set the example of genuine character and took the punch when rejection and foul play took its course against Him. God's love sometimes seems crazy and outrageous because it is. In thinking about what Jesus did for us, we should remember that Jesus didn't abandon the process of doing what was right in the face of wrong. I'm convinced that the self-control of God against our sin represents the love of God. We should be thankful that God didn't throw a temper tantrum and kill us. Unlike Him we can sometimes be biased and revengeful when we are hurt. Despite our anger we must lean on God and ask Him for the help to become better. With all people we must do our best to fix our wrongs and to try and live at peace.

Romans 12:18

18 If it is possible, as far as it depends on you, live at peace with everyone.

God wants us to learn how to better control ourselves and to use wisdom when offense or wrong come our way. Being angry about something or someone can lead us to bigger problems, and we must be careful not to live trapped in a problem. Anger and offense are often the opportunity for the devil to enter into our lives and heart.

Ephesians 4:26–27

26 Be angry and do not sin; do not let the sun go down on your anger, 27 and give no opportunity to the devil.

Reflection

Do you ever get mad? If so how do you handle it? Today, I want to encourage you to discuss this devotion with someone and ask how they think God would want them to deal with anger. Study and let God minister to you.

Prayer

Father God, please help me to better myself and to trust in You. When I am angry, help me not to sin against you but to pray and fix my attitude. You desire unity and peace in Christ Jesus, so please help me to demonstrate Your will in my life. In Jesus name I pray. Amen.

Scripture

Proverbs 14:29

"Whoever is slow to anger has great understanding,
but he who has a hasty temper exalts folly."

James 1:20

"for the anger of man does not produce the righteousness of God."

Day 42

Fairness

Not everything in your life is going to be fair. Unfortunately, life is just not fair. Some people are born with decent parents while others are born to drug-addicted parents. Some people are born wealthy while others struggle in poverty. Some people have athletic abilities while other people struggle with Everyday disabilities. Some people have worked hard for their possessions while other people rob for their possessions. The bottom line is that life isn't always about fairness but about character. God knows all about the problems of the world, yet He still reminds us not to be entangled but to take heart.

2 Timothy 2:3–4

3 "Join with me in suffering, like a good soldier of Christ Jesus. 4 No one serving as a soldier gets entangled in civilian affairs, but rather tries to please his commanding officer."

John 16:33

33 "I have told you these things, so that in me you may have peace. In this world you will have trouble. But take heart! I have overcome the world."

Jesus knew what it was like to be poorly treated, and the truth is that there will be times when others will poorly mistreat us. Things may not look fair at times, but if the exchange of our sufferings help lead us to Christ, then I promise you that the exchange is good. God knows what's best.

Romans 5:3–5

³ "Not only that, but we rejoice in our sufferings, knowing that suffering produces endurance, ⁴ and endurance produces character, and character produces hope, ⁵ and hope does not put us to shame, because God's love has been poured into our hearts through the Holy Spirit who has been given to us."

When our pains don't seem fair or the tragedies of the world cause us grief, we must remember to look to the healer of the world: Jesus Christ. At the cross Jesus has shown us what unfairness looks like and at the same time what love, character, and the power of faith and obedience are all about. The enemy would love to terrorize us through pain and tragedy, while

God desires to heal and govern us through the hope and trust found in Jesus Christ. God has given this world to us as a gift, and the effects of our sins continue to distort it. God is not at fault for the unfairness of the world, but He loves us enough to help us and to give us a fighting chance for heaven through Christ Jesus. We all have a shared responsibility to learn and grow in the events of hardship, but more importantly, the victory belongs to those who stick it out.

Matthew 24:12–13

12 Because of the increase of wickedness, the love of most will grow cold, 13 but the one who stands firm to the end will be saved.

Reflection

When life is unfair, how do you deal with it? Do you give up, or do you turn to drugs or alcohol? Do you blame God or do you endure and cooperate with Him? Today, I want to encourage you to help change the world around you. Learn that we have a shared responsibly to help others and to pray for everyone. Things in life may be unfair, and for that very reason we need the help of God to restore and correct our hearts and minds.

Prayer

Father God, we pray for our world toDay that You would continue to show mercy and love on in a global way as well as a personal way. Thank you for character building and the breath of life. May we learn to care as You would and to grow from selfishness to helpfulness. In your name I pray. Amen.

Scripture

2 Corinthians 1:3–4

3 "Blessed be the God and Father of our Lord Jesus Christ, the Father of mercies and God of all comfort, 4 who comforts us in all our affliction, so that we may be able to comfort those who are in any affliction, with the comfort with which we ourselves are comforted by God."

Day 43

Silence

Have you ever been quiet about something that you felt should be heard? If it was edifying, then what held you back? Oftentimes we become hesitant when we should be bold. Sometimes fear or pride can hold us back when it shouldn't. In some situations, it may be wise to keep silent, but in other situations, it may cause trouble and harm when we don't speak up. Even Esther in the Bible was confronted about not speaking up when trouble was coming for the Israelites.

Esther 4:14

14 For if you remain silent at this time, relief and deliverance for the Jews will arise from another place, but you and your father's family will perish. And who knows but that you have come to your royal position for such a time as this?"

When the responsibility comes to speak up on issues that God puts on our heart to address, then we are held accountable for that. To avoid conflict through silence is sometimes criminal in itself. You don't have to be a pastor, evangelist, or activist to speak up in times of trouble. Instead you need to have the conviction, leading, and willingness of a servant of God to effectively do what's right. God knows the situation at hand, and if He didn't want you to know, then He could have very easily kept you from knowing. Regardless of our status or position in life, our integrity to do right is what counts. Sometimes trouble could be prevented in the bravery of a conversation.

Reflection

Have you ever had a hard but necessary conversation with someone? Did you learn something and could you have done something better? At times we are too silent in matters that need to be discussed. ToDay I want to encourage you to speak up on issues needing to be addressed in a Christ like manner. When the time is right, do what's right.

Prayer

Father God, please forgive me for anytime that I was supposed to have addressed but didn't. Help me toDay to do what's right going forward. Let me not be prideful or arrogant but gentle and humble in my approach and with the love that you share with me. May the meditation of my heart find delight in Your sight. In Jesus name I pray. Amen!

Scripture

Colossians 4:6

6 "Let your speech always be gracious, seasoned with salt, so that you may know how you ought to answer each person."

Image

Have you ever dressed to impress? If so, did you trust that your image would give you favor or bring you attention? In the world we live in today, we often see celebrities on TV wearing fancy jewelry and dressing to impress. We see their style and listen to what they have to say. We may be curious about the image that they portray or what the latest trend is. As humans this is the kind of thing that many people have come to like, or else there wouldn't be so much money tied up into what we call celebrity or reality shows. However, this kind of thing is often dangerous when it feeds into people's ego, self-esteem, or value system. As Christians, our worth shouldn't be tied to the image or popularity of anyone. Our value comes from God. God is our example and role model, not the models or actors on TV. God is more glorious than what we can find in anyone else. Therefore, our trust shouldn't be in the fashion statements of people but in God.

1 Peter 3:3–4

3 "Do not let your adorning be external—the braiding of hair and the putting on of gold jewelry, or the clothing you wear—4 but let your adorning be the hidden person of the heart with the imperishable beauty of a gentle and quiet spirit, which in God's sight is very precious."

As Christians we are to be more modest about beauty, not lustful or arrogant. We should be a little more cautious about what we endorse when it comes to such things. Living after a reputation of flattery or self-worth is a dangerous thing.

Ezekiel 28:17

17 "Your heart was proud because of your beauty; you corrupted your wisdom for the sake of your splendor. I cast you to the ground; I exposed you before kings, to feast their eyes on you."

God knows our heart, and for some that is scary, but if we want change, we must come to Him for change. Overall, we are made in God's image (Gen. 1:27), and we must be careful to who we give glory to.

Reflection

Did today's devotion help you rethink what pop culture endorses? Do you deal with self-esteem issues? I want to encourage you to search the scripture for more answers. God deeply cares about where we place our attention and what we value. Rejoice that God cares and wants you to be a voice for His glory.

Prayer

Father God, I thank You for what you have done for me. May my trust be in You and not in the value system of this world. I ask for the desire of repentance in my heart if there be any idolatry in it. Clean me up and help me get what I need to get right for Your glory and my growth in Jesus name, I pray. Amen.

Scripture

2 Timothy 3:1–5

3 "But understand this, that in the last days there will come times of difficulty. 2 For people will be lovers of self, lovers of money, proud, arrogant, abusive, disobedient to their parents, ungrateful, unholy, 3 heartless, unappeasable, slanderous, without self-control, brutal, not loving good, 4 treacherous, reckless, swollen with conceit,

lovers of pleasure rather than lovers of God, 5 having the appearance of godliness, but denying its power. Avoid such people."

Day 45

Community Makes a Difference

D id you know that God tells us to do certain things through community?

Hebrews 10:24–25

24 "And let us consider how to stir up one another to love and good works, 25 not neglecting to meet together, as is the habit of some, but encouraging one another, and all the more as you see the Day drawing near."

God has always been serious about community. God cares that community happens and that it isn't forsaken or taken for granted. Oftentimes you will see in the Bible that God governs, guides, and protects through community. If it wasn't true, then God wouldn't have governed through Moses, Gideon or the Apostles. Neither would God have used angels to help exercise His will. The point is that God loves community. It is our responsibility to have a personal relationship with God, but it is also our responsibility to be involved with community. As believers, we need each other, and within our community we can discover God given gifts.

1 Peter 4:8–11

8 "Above all, keep loving one another earnestly, since love covers a multitude of sins. 9 Show hospitality to one another without grumbling. 10 As each has received a gift, use it to serve one another, as good stewards of God's varied grace: 11 whoever speaks, as one who speaks oracles of God; whoever serves, as one who serves by the strength that God supplies—in order that in everything God may be glorified through Jesus Christ. To him belong glory and dominion forever and ever. Amen."

Yes, community can look messy sometimes, but even in God's wisdom, He still calls for community to happen. It is our job to help maintain it, and sometimes that is through a smile, a helping hand, a word of encouragement, a phone call, and so on and so forth. When community seems to get messy, we must remember that the devil is our enemy, not each other. We must make the effort to have respect and make the effort to achieve and maintain harmony.

Romans 12:16

16 "Live in harmony with one another. Do not be haughty, but associate with the lowly. Never be wise in your own sight."

In the sense of a courtroom I like to say, if it takes a community to convict a person, then it will take a community to help restore a person.

If we want to make change, then we need each other. God cares that we have community.

Reflection

Have you ever made an excuse not to go to church? If so, was your reason good enough for God to agree with you? Today, I want to encourage you to get involved with the community of your church if you have a home church. If not then I want to encourage you to look for a home church. Join in on the unity of community and ask God to help you to fit in the way He wants you to fit in.

Prayer

Father God, I pray for the church communities around the world to grow and to love like You would want us to love. May Your glorious and holy name be lifted up. Thank you for what you are doing through the power of community, and may we get to be a part of that in honor of You and for Your glory. If anyone needs to forgive someone in the body of Christ, then please help that person to forgive and may that person be set free. If anyone has been hurt by community, then please help restore that person and use that person to help strengthen others. In Jesus name I pray. Amen.

Scripture

Proverbs 27:17

17 "Iron sharpens iron, and one man sharpens another."

Sandra Tarlen
Rejection and Forgiveness

By
Ricky Lopez

Sometimes God puts special people in our life even when we don't know why or what will come from it. For me, Sandra was one of those special people that God put in my life. When I was twenty years old, I met Sandra while in prison. Sandra had been volunteering in prison ministry for years and still does.

With an uncommon testimony Sandra caught my attention. At a young age Sandra had to endure a very physical and emotional childhood.

By the age of four years old, Sandra was playing near a pit fire and a little boy flung gasoline across the fire where Sandra was sitting. In moments Sandra's life changed, and she would no longer be the same, as her face was caught in flames. Sandra suffered 1st, 2nd and 3rd degree burns, never allowing her childhood to be normal again.

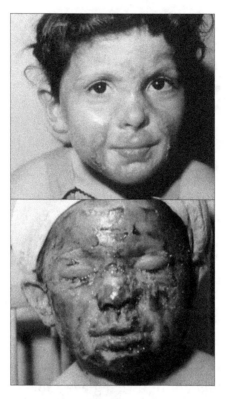

Growing up, Sandra was rejected and looked at differently by the other kids she grew up with. Although Sandra wanted the affection that any little girl might want, she did not get it. The idea to be loved and treated like a princess was far from her reality. Eventually this would lead to problems. In search for affection and acceptance, Sandra found comfort in the generosity of an elderly man who was a carpenter and had a workshop nearby. The elderly man built doll furniture for Sandra, but it later came with a price to pay. Sandra would soon be introduced to porn magazines and then molested. For several years this went on. Sandra desired a common childhood like the other kids around her and when she didn't get to experience one, it affected her deeply. To people around her, Sandra stuck out like a sore thumb and there was nothing she could really do about it.

By the age of twelve, Sandra was walking home from an event when four men pulled over to offer her a ride. Being noticed and wanting to be accepted, Sandra said yes, but once again there would be a price to pay. The four men took her to a trailer and gang raped her and treated her like trash. Not only had Sandra been scarred for life from her burns and deeply hurt by the rejection of others but now this! Back at home her mother blamed her and sent her to live in another state. Unfortunately, that wasn't the answer or solution that Sandra needed. Sandra was in need of God, loving parents, and a community that cared for her, but that wasn't what she was getting.

As Sandra began to date and she ended up marrying several different times thinking that she could escape life through romance.

By sixteen, Sandra was married and had a child. However, this marriage didn't last very long. Sandra thought that she could leave her problems behind by marring someone in the military and living on a military base overseas. While there Sandra ran into an old schoolmate and realized that it doesn't matter how far you run, your issues will always follow and effect you when you don't learn how to deal with them. Later her military marriage ended. In need of the true Love that only God can offer and heal a person with, Sandra continued live unnourished and sought for acceptance in the wrong places. Unlike most people Sandra had to deal with people constantly staring at her and making judgment or comments about her because of the way she looked from the scares of her childhood. For anyone that is not an easy thing to go through.

Again Sandra married with hope that things might work out. However, while working one Day Sandra's new husband tricked Sandra into signing certain legal documents and sold their home and ran away to Vegas. In her new husbands pursuit of fulfilling his own life with happiness, he lost everything and left Sandra high and dry. By this time Sandra was left with nothing but more scars, but now the scars were inside her heart. That marriage was annulled. With few to no breaks in life, Sandra kept moving forward, but things felt miserable. By age twenty-five Sandra married again in hope that a new relationship could be a new start. Unfortunately, a new marriage or the affection of a new spouse wasn't the answer that she was in need of. This marriage did not work out either and was over in just a few months. Having experienced major hardships and after gone through many major surgeries by this time, Sandra's need for a savior became more evident.

In some of Sandra's hardship she had wrote this poem:

"I'm not me' I'm not what you see. I'm in a shell and it feels like hell. I don't run; I don't laugh; I don't have fun. I want out. I want free. I want to be me."

Sandra knew that there had to be more to life than what she was living. Around this time Sandra was invited by a friend to a Christian conference. After contemplation Sandra decided to go and was compelled to what the speaker was saying. As the word of God entered into Sandra's mind and heart, Sandra went to go talk with the speaker of the conference and it lead to her accepting Jesus Christ as Lord and savior of her life. It was there and then that Sandra would be forever changed. As a new Christian she had a new challenge on the rise. For years Sandra had been hurt by different people, and none of them deserved her forgiveness, but in the face of the cross she realized that she didn't deserve the Lord's forgiveness either. In this crossroad of life and new challenge, Sandra decided to forgive and to love in place of all the hurt that she had experienced. Sandra truly traded in her sorrow for a joy that can only come from God. No longer would Sandra need to search for acceptance from others or to let rejection control her. Although there was a process to growing as a Christian, Sandra was all in and was soon to be tested. While volunteering to help children who had been physically burned in life, a doctor convinced Sandra to have more surgeries. However, she was told that the process would be difficult and at one point she would have large noticeable cheeks.

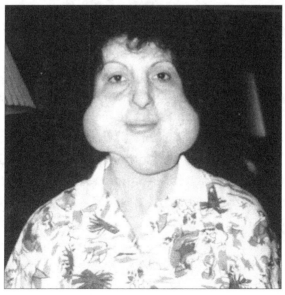

Sandra decided to go through the process of surgeries, but once again she would be looked at roughly and judged by others around her. In the process of the surgeries the feeling of embarrassment and rejection came back strongly as people starred at her and questioned why she looked like that. While at work one day, Sandra went out into the mall where two young men passed by and one hocked a mouthful of spit in Sandra's face because how she looked. In complete shock and hurt Sandra went to the basement of her office and prayed for strength and the emotional pain that the young man had caused her. As Sandra was praying, the Lord began to minister to her. In the rejection, hurt, and sadness, the Lord reminded Sandra of those that persecuted Him and spit in His face. It was in that moment that Sandra realized she had a choice to make. Sandra gathered the strength of her faith in Jesus and decided to forgive the young man for what he did. Sandra was given the option to leave work that day, but she stayed. A short time later the same young man who spit in her face approached her and apologized. — Sandra told him that he was forgiven.

Today, Sandra is a biblical disciple and helps to counsel others in need of healing. Sandra volunteers in the prisons and continues to help others find healing through the real love and hope found in Jesus Christ. Sandra has had the opportunity to lead many to the Lord and continues to teach others about forgiveness. Sandra has not only been able to overcome these hard issues in life, but she was also able to lead her dad and mother to the Lord. Sandra would encourage all of us to rethink what forgiveness means and would challenge us to deal with any unforgiveness we might be holding onto. The price that comes through unforgiveness is not worth the hurt and pain of emotional scars. Sometimes we have to learn to let go of our pain and decide to help stop the cycle of the prison that unforgiveness brings us.

Matthew 6:14–15 English Standard Version (ESV)

[14] "For if you forgive others their trespasses, your heavenly Father will also forgive you, [15] but if you do not forgive others their trespasses, neither will your Father forgive your trespasses."

As mentioned before, Sandra is one of those special people that comes into a person's life and really helps them to rethink the power behind forgiveness. To this day Sandra continues to live out the gospel and goes into the prisons to help make the world a better place. Regardless of her age, gender, scars, or past, Sandra can truly remind us to forgive and to move forward when we feel like the victim. We should all learn to handle rejection better and not to chase after the acceptance of man's approval but the approval of God who wants us to be set free from the pain that this world can bring.

May you have enjoyed the reading of this book and may it be used as a tool of growth in Christ Jesus. When in doubt or trouble, remember that Jesus is the answer to the problem.

E-mail: rickylopez4christ@gmail.com

CPSIA information can be obtained
at www.ICGtesting.com
Printed in the USA
BVHW041958260422
635379BV00011B/439

9 781631 297212